DON'T FORGET YOUR ROOTS

SARAH ROUTHIER

DISCLAIMER

The author is not a health care professional or mental health professional. The contents of this book are for informational purposes only. While the information and opinions found in this book are written based on information available at the time of writing, and are believed to be accurate according to the best discernment of the author, the content is not intended to be a substitute for professional medical advice, diagnosis, or treatment. Any health concern must be assessed by a doctor. If you think you require assessment, call your doctor or local emergency department immediately. Any information provided by the author or the contents of this book is solely for the purpose of expressing the individual experience.

If you, or anyone you know, is contemplating suicide - call the Suicide Prevention Service:

In Canada: 1-833-456-4566

In U.S.A.: 1-800-273-8255

I would like to dedicate this book to all First Responders who selflessly sacrifice themselves to serve their communities. You are heroes.

To anyone who has lost a loved one to suicide. I hope you find your roots and this brings you peace, comfort, and inspiration.

With immense love and support, I dedicate this to Jacob, Nicholas, and Emily. Please always remember how much Daddy loved you, he will always live within you, and don't forget your roots.

CONTENTS

INTRODUCTION

Monday and Tuesday, July 30th - 31st, 2018

It seemed like a normal Monday, just like any other Monday during summer break. While I went to work, Sylvain stayed home to be with our kids. We were often able to coordinate our work schedules since he was a shift worker and I wasn't so when the kids were off school for the summer, one of us stayed home with them while the other worked.

This summer was a bit different since Sylvain was on sick leave. Nothing was out of the ordinary that day. Work, unpack from the weekend at the trailer, dinner, clean the kitchen, put the kids to sleep, and have some quiet time to ourselves. We would talk about our days, about the funny things the kids did, about what happened at work, and what our plans for the next day would be. It was the exact same routine we had for years. I could never have anticipated what was to come in the following days.

Our days were filled with the kids' activities, sports, swimming, and weekend trips to our trailer at the lake. We took summer vacations to visit our parents who lived a few hours away, did day trips to local beaches and nearby cities, wanting the kids to visit the zoos, aquariums, and have many summer memories. For all intents and purposes, we were the typical All-Canadian family. Two working parents, three active kids.

We lived in a comfortable house in the country, with a two-car garage, a sunny kitchen, the children each had a room of their own. We had built our home five years prior, choosing the lot because of the large private backyard that was perfect to build an outdoor rink in the winter for the kids.

While we didn't have a white picket fence, like the American Dream, we did have a large private backyard where we often had family games of baseball, and campfires at night on those summer evenings, and an annual outdoor hockey game in the winter with all the kids' hockey teammates.

We were blessed in so many ways and we had a perfect life. Some would even think we were the picture of an ideal family. Heck, even I thought we were the picture of the ideal family. I often thought that our life was too good to be true and it was just a matter of time before we got handed a trial or tribulation. There's no way we could just keep going through life without something difficult occurring. Would it be someone we loved getting cancer? Maybe one of our parents would announce a divorce? Maybe Sylvain would get injured at work? Please, don't let anything happen to my kids I would pray. Life is about bumps in the road and how we handle them, but I never expected the bump that was coming.

As we went to bed that Monday night, Sylvain listened to a meditation podcast as I brushed my teeth and got ready.

It was his latest attempt at unwinding from the stress, one of the many recommendations made by the therapist he was seeing. I laid down in front of him on a weird angle, so we were facing each other and held his hand. His wedding ring was between his fingers as I played with it and spun it around on his ring finger. I stared into his eyes and could see the exhaustion from this man I loved so much and kissed him goodnight.

An hour later, Sylvain was snoring so incredibly loud that it woke me up. At first, I was a little annoyed that it had woken me since I had to get up early for work the next morning but then I started giggling. I got out my cell phone and recorded the sound because I thought he would get a kick out of hearing himself and how loud he was the next morning. Eventually, I couldn't fall back to sleep, so I nudged him awake and asked him to go sleep in the spare bedroom in the basement because he was keeping me awake with his snoring. Without hesitation, he got up, grabbed a backpack he had beside the bed and went to the basement.

The next morning, I got ready for work and let him sleep in since he hadn't been sleeping well. I left him a note on the kitchen counter to call me when he woke up. The kids were already awake, helping themselves to cereal and morning tv shows. I told Jacob, our oldest son, that if they needed anything, to go wake up daddy. He was sleeping in the spare bedroom in the basement. I left for work with a strange nagging feeling that I tried to ignore.

By mid-morning, I hadn't heard from them yet, so I called Sylvain to see if he was awake. This wasn't unusual for us. Throughout our relationship, we were used to checking in with each other throughout the day, even while at work. So, I thought nothing of it. When I asked what his plans for the day were, he said he was going to hang out at the house for the morning and then take the kids down to the harbour and go fishing. I knew the kids would be so excited to do this with their dad and it sounded like they were going to have a lovely day without me. Part of me wished that I could be home with them too, but I knew I only had a few more days of work, and then I would have a week off with them. Just get through this work week! We agreed we would meet after work later that afternoon.

We had been planning on selling our house in the country and buying a new house from a builder in the suburbs. We decided we were going to meet at the builder's office at 4:30 pm that day to officially put in the offer on our new house. I was very excited since we had been talking about this move for weeks. We researched the perfect location so the kids wouldn't have to switch schools, picked out a lot in a beautiful neighbourhood that backed onto green space, choose a layout that was smaller than our current home, but gave the kids their own space in the basement. The new house represented a new future for us, where we could leave the inconvenience and stress of country living behind.

Our phone conversation was off. I could tell Sylvain was not himself. He was quiet and didn't say too much. I had to lead the conversation and ask questions. I asked him if he wanted me to send him the house plans again to review before our meeting with the builder. He said yes please, in his cute French accent. I told him I would arrange for him to drop the kids off with my brother so we could have a meeting with the builder without the kids. I asked him if everything was alright and he said yes, he was just tired. As I was on the phone with him, a lifeguard peeked her head in my office and said there is a patron asking to speak to me. I told Sylvain I needed to go, and I would see him at 4:30 pm.

That was the last conversation I had with him.

Around 2:30 that afternoon, I got a text from my brother – *"Is everything ok with Sylvain?"*

I answered – *"Yes, why?"*

He said Sylvain dropped off the kids at his house before lunchtime, with the excuse that he had to go to work to fill out some paperwork and that he would be right back.

I was really confused because that was not the plan when I talked to Sylvain. He never mentioned anything about needing to fill out more paperwork when I spoke to him. This was odd since I had attended the last work meeting the week prior with him and was keeping track of all the paperwork that was required. I tried calling him multiple times and he didn't answer his phone. I had sent him a text message, a Blackberry Messenger (BBM) to be exact, after our phone conversation reminding him that the boys needed new skates and if he could take them shopping after dinner and after our meeting with the builder, that would be great. He dealt with all the hockey stuff and knew how to get them the proper skates that they would need for the upcoming hockey season. With BBM, I could tell that he never read that message. This was very unusual behaviour for him.

I tried to ignore a pit that was forming in my stomach and kept typing at my computer. I tried calling him again. All sorts of thoughts and worries flooded my mind.

Where was he? Why would he go to work? Why can't I get a hold of him? Why would he lie to me about his plans today? Why would he drop the kids off with my brother and leave?

None of it made sense. Yet, in my heart, there was only

one answer that I could think of, and I simply wouldn't let myself think of *that*.

I called my supervisor in a panic. I blurted out to her that I couldn't get a hold of Sylvain, there is something wrong, and I needed to go home right away. I texted my brother that I would go to the house and see if he was there. He must have stopped at home and fallen asleep.

I walked out of work and noticed that our family van was in the staff parking lot, which was strange because that morning, I had driven his car to work. He must have switched vehicles with me for some odd reason. This all made no sense. Normally, he would have told me he was switching cars and he would have come into my workplace to say hello. Luckily, my keychain had both sets of car keys on it.

I got a huge knot in my stomach as I drove home. I kept trying to call his phone and left several messages.

When I got to our house, his car was not in our driveway. That was another sign that something was off. I thought of going directly to my brother's house and waiting for him to show up there, but something propelled me to go into our home and look around. It was eerily quiet since I rarely was home without the noise, hustle and bustle of the kids of three kids yelling or running around. The sun was shining through the large living room windows, and I could tell Sylvain spent his morning cleaning the house. It was spotless and everything was in its place. I could smell something from the kitchen. Sylvain had prepared a chicken that was cooking in the crockpot for dinner. As I walked down the hallway towards our bedroom, I yelled "Sylvain are you here?". I'm not sure why I called out since I knew he obviously wasn't home since his car wasn't in the driveway. I slowly walked into our bedroom. The bed was made, clothes were picked up off the floor and put away and in the direct centre on our bed was a hand-written note. I recognized Sylvain handwriting right away. I started to cry and panic.

I knew exactly what it was even before I read it.

He left me a suicide note.

FIRST COMES LOVE

The first time I met Sylvain, I was on my way home from a bar in Valleyfield, Quebec. It was an interesting encounter to say the least.

In Ontario, the legal drinking age is 19. Across the border, in Quebec, it's 18. Many of us teenagers who lived in Ontario, but close to the Quebec border, would drive across the border, just to go to the bars. *The Saint*, was a bar just past the Quebec border and it was the place to go for multiple reasons. Firstly, it was only a 30-minute drive from our town. Secondly, the cover charge was only five dollars. Thirdly, the drinks only cost one dollar each. So, for us 18-year-olds, with twenty dollars in our pocket, we could have a really great night! The biggest reason we liked to go there is that we could meet new people there that were from other places other than our little town.

When my friends made plans to go to Quebec on any given Saturday night, I was often the driver. Not only because I had my own car, that my brother and I shared, but also because I didn't really like to drink too much. I'm not sure what my parents did to ingrain that trait in me, but I hope I can pass it onto my own kids. So, for most of that year, I was the designated driver on our Saturday nights at *The Saint*.

We would get to the bar around 10:30 at night, and it would be packed with all kinds of people. They played mostly techno music all night, the drum and bass so loud that it would be ringing in your ears even hours after you got home. The bar was dark, with strobe lights flashing. Sometimes, it was hard to make out the people you knew and the people who were strangers. In those days, smoking was allowed in bars, so, on top of it being dark and loud, it was also smoke-filled. Nonetheless, *The Saint* was our teenaged Saturday night refuge.

I don't remember too much about the particular Saturday night that I met Sylvain after the bar closed. Like most Saturday nights, my friends and I stayed until the music ended, the lights came on, and the bar staff would try to kick everyone out at three in the morning. That was another bonus to the bars in Quebec, they stayed open until very late at night. Our usual routine was to stop on our way home at a Wendy's that was open all night along the high-way, so we could get some burgers for the rest of the drive home. This seemed to be everyone's routine for the drive back to Cornwall. Often, you would run into people you didn't even realize were at the same bar as you.

I was walking back to the car with all my girlfriends in it when I ran into an old friend, Nathan. We hadn't seen each other for a decade. Our younger brothers played hockey together as kids and we knew who each other was from getting dragged to all their games. I was amazed he recognized me, and that I recognized him. As we talked, we realized that we had both been at *The Saint* that night. He said he was and went with a bunch of guys from his brother's hockey team and, in fact, they were also on my brother's current team. At age 18, I no longer went to watch my brother play hockey since I didn't really care, but as a few of the guys from the team gathered around him, I realized they were no longer little boys, they had become handsome young men.

He proceeded to introduce me to the guys on my brother's team. "This is Ryan..." he pointed to each guy in turn, "Jon... Dominic... ", as he pointed to the guy furthest away, behind the picnic table, puking his guts out, he said, "and that, over there, is Sylvain."

I thought - *Oh geez, poor him, that must be awful.* Never in my wildest dreams did I think that would be the moment I met the love of my life, my future husband and the father to my children - life works in mysterious ways. That night marked the first time I knew he existed.

A few weeks went by, and I kept running into the hockey guys at school. The hockey guys, including my brother Jamie, played for the Akwesasne Wolves, a Junior B hockey team that was for 16 to 21-year-olds. Most of them wanted to make it to the Junior A Cornwall Colts team and eventually get a university scholarship to play hockey in the United States.

My high school was a fairly new catholic secondary school with about 600 students which was attached to a public high school. Our two schools shared the auditorium and the cafeteria. Sometime this would cause problems because kids from the two schools would often bump heads and fights would break out in shared hallways or the cafeteria. The cafeteria is where I saw the hockey boys a lot. My friend Kelly and I were definitely intrigued by them. Many of them moved to our small town just to play hockey which meant new blood and they were definitely tall, muscular, athletic and good looking. I instantly had a crush on the one named Dominic. He was tall, charming, had a great smile and exuded a very intriguing confidence.

Some of the hockey guys, Kelly and myself, quickly figured out that we all had a spare at the same time. The hangout spot was the shared cafeteria so often during our spare, we would play cards, chat, and get to know each other. I got to meet Sylvain again under sober circumstances. He had bleached blonde hair although I knew his natural hair colour must have been a dark brown. He had dark brown eyes, a shy smile and loved to show us card tricks. He had broken English, with a very strong French accent, and initially I thought he must be indigenous Canadian. He had the same accent as the majority of students that went to the public high school and played hockey for the Akwesasne Wolves, which was an indigenous team. He once told me that he was French and grew up in Montreal which was cool to me because I could speak French and would often practice with him.

Sylvain grew up in Montreal to a very loving family and had two younger siblings who idolized him. He was very active and very smart. He quickly excelled at hockey and was drafted to play hockey at the young age of 15 and his goal was to get a university scholarship to play hockey at an American university. This proved quite difficult if you didn't know how to speak English. So, he decided to move to Ontario from Quebec to play hockey, learn English, and pursue his dreams. He played hockey for many Junior teams in Eastern Ontario, and he was billeted (meaning, he would be hosted by families as a guest in their home for the hockey season) by some wonderful families, which later had a huge impact on him and our family.

Sylvain started asking me questions about Kelly and

told me he definitely had an interest in her. I told him I had an interest in his friend Dominic and we got to work trying to set each other up.

The irony was, Kelly let me know, gently, that she had no interest in Sylvain. When I broke the news to him, he told me the same about Dominic not having an interest in me either. I guess it was not meant to be. Kelly and I hung out with the hockey boys often and went to cheer them on at their hockey games. We all became good friends until one night at *The Saint*, it all changed.

On a typical Saturday evening in November, we went to watch the hockey boys play hockey. We cheered for all the hockey boys that were playing, including my brother.

My friend Jen, Kelly, and I, planned to go to *The Saint* after the game with the hockey boys. The plan was to meet at Sylvain and Jon's billet family's house after the game. Then one of them would drive us to my house so I could drop off my car.

For once, I didn't have to be the designated driver. Jen wasn't allowed out after the hockey game, but before I dropped her off at home, we stopped at the house the hockey guys' lived in. Jen was in the passenger seat beside me, with Kelly in the backseat. While we waited for one of the guys to come out to the driveway to tell us the plan, we talked about the typical teenaged girl stuff - who we were going to see at the club, what we were wearing, who was interested in who. Sylvain came out freshly showered, to tell me that they were ready to leave, and would follow me in another car to my place so that I could drop off my car.

As we headed towards my house to drop Jen off, she looked at me, her eyes wide, and said, "Wow, he is so good-looking, and you are so lucky that you are going out to *The Saint* with him tonight."

When Jen said that to me, it was like a giant lightbulb went off in my head – "Oh my goodness, she is right!". Sylvain was really good-looking, but, I had never thought of him in that way because we were just friends, and I was trying to set him up with Kelly. I instantly got nervous and excited about what might lie ahead for the evening.

I dropped Jen off at my house for her to get her car and the boy's car followed me home. When I jumped into the boys' car, Sylvain wasn't in it, and I was disappointed that I wasn't going to ride with him to the bar. I was worried that maybe he changed his mind and decided not to go at all. I tried to sound as casual as possible when I asked where Sylvain had ended up and Jon said he jumped in with someone else. For the whole car ride to *The Saint*, I kept thinking about Sylvain and how I was now attracted to him and was thinking of him more than just a friend. After all, he was really funny, super sweet, a genuine really nice guy and had a gorgeous smile. I was praying that he was going to be there when we arrived.

We got to the bar, I walked in and instantly started sweeping the place trying to find Sylvain. A huge feeling of relief came over me when I saw him. He already had a drink in his hand. I went up to him, gave him a hug and said, "I'm so glad you're here".

With the loud music and the low lights, I could tell he was surprised, but he smelled really good. I was surprised by my sudden attraction. He was wearing jeans, a plaid shirt that he left open to the black t-shirt he was wearing underneath. I had to reach on my tippy toes to hug him. At six-foot-two, he towered over me, and had large broad shoulders. It felt good to be in his arms, and he must have felt something shift between us too. He said he was happy I was there too and asked me if I wanted a drink. We went over to the bar, I ordered two lime vodka drinks, one for each hand, and we hit the dance floor.

At first, we danced a little far from each other, whispering jokes in each other's ears, mostly about other people we were observing. Once he finished his drinks and had his hands free, he put his arms around my waist and gently pulled me closer to him. The techno music was pounding and so was my heart. We danced for a while and at one point I realized we hadn't even seen any of our friends that we came with. We were on the middle of the dance floor, and it felt like everyone else around us disappeared. All I could think about or concentrate on was Sylvain. We went and got a couple more drinks and went back to dancing. The night seemed to go by so fast, yet I can remember every detail. Even today, over 20 years later, I can recall it like it was yesterday.

At the end of the night, we were still dancing, and a slow song came on. We slowed our pace as he pulled me close to him. I could smell his cologne and he gently placed his cheek against mine. As if in slow motion, I could feel him move his mouth slowly grazing the side of my cheek until our lips met. He kissed me softly and we couldn't stop kissing. The lights came on and we were still kissing. We kissed the whole way home in the back of our friend's car, and we stood in my driveway trying to say goodbye and kept kissing.

I knew from that moment, that I never wanted to stop kissing Sylvain.

We started dating and eventually Kelly and Dominic started dating too. I guess you could say we totally swapped love interests. We became a couple within a wider circle of friends.

One thing I didn't expect, was how mad my brother was at me. I had never experienced my brother being so angry with me. He said I could have any guy in Cornwall that I wanted so why did I have to date one on his hockey team. I'm sure Jamie endured some teasing and dressing room talk that made Sylvain and I dating extremely uncomfortable for him. Thankfully, he got over it and they became really close friends. They used to call each other "brothers from different mothers."

Christmas came and I was able to go visit his family with him in Montreal. I had met them before from times they had come to his hockey games. They were very nice and very French. He was excited to show me around Montreal and one evening he brought me to the top of Mont Royal. Mont Royal is a large mountain in the middle of the city that is actually a dormant volcano. The view from the top at night is so incredibly breathtaking. You can see all the lights of the city from miles away and I had never seen anything like it before in my life. I told Sylvain that if he ever decides to propose to someone someday, he should do it here. It was incredibly romantic.

It was our senior year of high school, and Sylvain and I went to prom together. Shortly after, his hockey season ended, and he moved back to Montreal to work for the summer. He got a job working with the City of Montreal giving out parking tickets and planned on starting police foundations at Maisonneuve College also in Montreal. I was a pool supervisor and lifeguard for the City of Cornwall, and we spent our weekends going back and forth from Montreal and Cornwall so we could see each other. I was going to attend Algonquin College in Ottawa after the summer to study Nursing.

Making a long-distance relationship work was not easy. We spent many hours on the phone each day talking, and I would cry a lot because I missed him so much. Eventually we did the two-and-a-half-hour commute back and forth between Montreal and Ottawa. Sylvain bought a car, and I would get on the Greyhound bus as we took turns spending weekends in Montreal and Ottawa. Goodbyes were painful and the long days waiting to see each other seemed to go on forever.

It definitely brought us closer as a couple because we cherished the moments, we were together and longed for the days we got to see each other again. Other than school, we enjoyed camping, going to see movies, hanging out with our friends, discovering the different bars and nightlife of both Ottawa and Montreal. Sylvain still played hockey in Montreal, and I enjoyed going to his games and cheering him on. We concentrated on school, and I eventually switch programs to Dental Assisting.

After a year-and-a-half of doing the long-distance thing, we couldn't make it work anymore and Sylvain decided to move to Ottawa so we could finally be together. He was able to switch to the Police Foundations program at Algonquin without losing his year of his schooling from Maisonneuve. We moved in together, finished our diplomas and quickly found jobs in Ottawa.

I started working as a Dental Assistant for a dentist and Sylvain got a job working at the House of Commons. This meant he was going to be working security at the Parliament buildings in Ottawa. He was really excited about getting his first job. He made lots of new friends, played on the Parliament hockey team and was quickly promoted to the Prime Minister's detail. This meant he was the Prime Minister's bodyguard anytime he was in the Parliament buildings. He wore a suit, carried a concealed gun, and had an earpiece in his ear so he could talk to his colleagues. They would walk in a formation of two guys in front of the Prime Minister and two guys behind. They needed to know where he was going in the building at all times so they could escort him around. Jean Chretien and Paul Martin were the Prime Ministers during the years that Sylvain worked at Parliament. Sylvain needed to know the Parliament buildings inside and out and although he enjoyed his job immensely, he found it boring. He would complain that nothing exciting ever happened at work and wanted to become a Police Officer.

2

THEN COMES MARRIAGE

After a few years of dating, I knew I was so in love with Sylvain and that I wanted to spend the rest of my life with him. I did not want to give him up and could not imagine my days without him. He was such a kind person, so loving, funny, and would do anything for me. He was never particularly good at expressing his feelings or emotions towards me, but I knew I meant a lot to him. We enjoyed our time off work with each other by going out with our friends, going to the movies, going on camping trips, small little vacations away renting cottages or visiting our families. We went boating, to the beaches, day trips exploring, and golfing together. We would take turns doing romantic things for each other such as cooking special dinners or surprise evenings at home dressing up and slow dancing in our living room. We did not have very much money, but the best thing was that love did not cost anything.

I knew early on that someday he would make an amazing dad from the way he interacted with little kids, which I saw when we were around his younger cousins.

Instinctively, he would get down on the ground and play with them, tickle them, and try to make them smile or laugh anyway he could think of. I often imagined him with our own kids or holding our baby someday and it would make me feel even more in love with him.

We started talking about the possibility of getting married and he was hesitant because we were so young. Honestly, I wanted to lock him down more than he liked the idea of getting married. None of our friends were married yet, and we worried if our families would approve. I wondered if I may have talked him into getting engaged or pressured him into proposing even though he was not ready. He always just wanted to make me happy so he would give in to what I wanted.

I was not 100% convinced that he would know how to propose, how to make it romantic or what type of ring to buy, so we went ring shopping together. I picked out the engagement ring that I loved even though we did not have money to pay for it, so Sylvain paid for it on his student line of credit. After we left the store, we stopped to see a movie and I was so nervous that he would forget the specially wrapped bag somewhere in the movie theatre.

Not too long after purchasing the engagement ring we made plans to go to Montreal to visit Sylvain's family. We planned out our engagement and how we were going to tell our families. I knew I wanted him to propose on the top of Mount Royal liked I had mentioned to him a few years earlier when he took me there for the first time. The first time we were there, I never thought I would be the woman he would be proposing to. I just wanted to let him know that someday when he decided to ask someone special to marry him, that this would be an incredibly romantic place to do it. We were only 18 years old at the time and I honestly did not think that would be it for dating for me but here we were 3 years later, and he was going to ask me to marry him.

We were at Sylvain's parents' house and had plans later that day to go for a drive to Mount Royal. Before we left, Sylvain told his brother he wanted to show him something. He brought his brother into the bathroom as I was in the living room beside and all of a sudden, I heard a clang hit the bathroom floor. I knew he was showing him the engagement ring and had dropped it. I held my breath hoping it did not fall down an air vent or something. Sylvain poked his head out of the bathroom because he knew I was probably worried and smiled at me holding the ring. He said: "Don't worry, I still got it!" I could not help but laugh because he did have clumsy moments and I knew I would not stop worrying about the safety of the ring until it was safe on my finger.

Later that day we started driving to the top of Mount Royal. We had to park halfway up and then walk the rest of the way. We were walking, holding hands, the sun was shining, and it was a crisp November day. I looked at Sylvain and we shared a few smiles, stopped walking a few times to exchange a kiss. We both knew in anticipation what was coming shortly and how this day would bring excitement and change our lives.

Sylvain looked a bit nervous once we got to the top. There was a large clearing at a look out point that was all done in stone, with gardens, sitting areas and a railing to prevent anyone from falling over. We walked over to get close to the railing which had the best view of the city below. The view was famous, with the skyline of buildings, the waterway, a bridge off in the distance. On a clear day, if you focused closely on details, you could make out people walking down the streets. You could even hear the bustle of the city, with people going about their day, even a siren and a police car with their lights on rushing through the busy streets.

We took in all that we could see and hear for a few minutes as he stood behind me and wrapped his arms around my waist. I could feel my heart beating out of my chest in anticipation and it took all my might to stop myself from giggling in excitement. Sylvain slowly turned me around, held both my hands, looked into my eyes, and pulled out a piece of paper from his coat pocket.

He got down on one knee and started reading off his piece of paper about how much I meant to him, how much he loved me and how much he wanted to spend the rest of his life with me. He pulled out the ring box with the ring safely in its spot, and asked me in his French accent: "Sarah, will you marry me and be my wife?"

I said yes, of course. I kissed him and hugged him. I was in shock that we actually just got engaged. I looked around to see if anyone had noticed what just happened but the busy tourists around us were paying more attention to the view than anything else.

I held the note he had handwritten and read the words a few more times. I loved his handwriting and wondered when had he taken the time to write down all his feelings for me. Other than small notes in cards for birthdays, Christmases, or anniversaries, this was the first time he gave me a love letter.

We rushed back to Sylvain's house and could not wait to tell his parents. We had it all planned out. I was nervous wondering if they would approve and what their reaction would be. Did they like me enough to be their daughter-in-law? Would they think this was a joke and we are too young?

Sylvain brought his parents into their room, and I

handed his mom a small box to open. It was almost Christmas time, so she was surprised that we were handing her an early gift. She opened the box and unwrapped a small Christmas ornament that was a bride and a groom standing on a small string. She did not look incredibly surprised and just said thank you in French and starting to leave to put it on the Christmas tree. She did not understand what we were trying to tell them. Sylvain said in French to his mom: "Mom were engaged."

His mom let out a small yell of excitement "Ohhhhh" and said "Felicitation", (Congratulations in French) and kissed Sylvain on both his cheeks, and then did the same to me. His dad shook Sylvain's hand, and kissed me on both my cheeks. They were happy for us and approved.

On our way back to Ottawa from Montreal, we planned on stopping at my parent's house in Cornwall to share our news. I was much more nervous to tell my parents than I was to tell his parents. I was their oldest child and only daughter and I would consider my upbringing to be somewhat strict in nature. After all we were only 21 years old and my plan was to tell them that we were not going to get married for another couple of years anyways.

We did the same thing with my parents as we did with Sylvain's and had them open a small Christmas ornament of a bride and groom. My parents figured out what it meant right away and completely shocked me with their excitement. I told my parents that we were going to wait a couple years before getting married since we were so young. They said: "Why? What's the point in waiting?" They said we were meant to be together and if we wanted to get married sooner, we had their blessing.

We decided to give ourselves about a year and a half to plan our wedding and chose a weekend in June that was a holiday in Quebec so Sylvain's family could travel to Ontario on a long weekend to come to the wedding. The date was set – June 26, 2004 – and I started working on all the plans.

Sylvain decided he also wanted his own engagement ring. I thought this was strange and never really heard of men wanting to wear an engagement ring before. He said: "Why not? You get to wear a ring to show that you are taken and are committed so I want to do the same." So, one day he bought himself a Sterling silver plain band so that everyone would know that he was taken as well. He wore his engagement ring proudly!

In the middle of wedding planning, I came across a huge wedding show that was happening on Ottawa, where we lived. There would be prizes, a chance to meet different vendors, a fashion show, basically everything we would need to plan out a wedding. Since my five bridesmaids lived far away or were busy and could not attend and I did not want to go on my own, I dragged Sylvain to the wedding show with me.

He was not overly impressed that he had to attend this event with me. There were hundreds of women with their wedding parties, all giddy and excited about the prospect of dress shopping, picking flowers and talking about Bachelorette parties. He was so upset with me for dragging him there because he felt so out of place and was not interesting in much of the wedding planning process, until the fashion show started.

Before the fashion show started, the organizers started to announce all the prizes that you could win for attending and filling out the ballot when we entered the show. Some of the prizes included winning all expenses paid for your entire wedding, winning a wedding dress of your dreams, winning an all-expense paid honeymoon or for all the grooms in the room, you could win 16 box tickets for an Ottawa Senators Hockey game.

Sylvain's eyes lit up as he looked at me and said: "Holy geez honey, there's no other guys here, so my chances of winning are really good!" Sure enough about a week later I got a phone call that Sylvain did indeed win the groom's grand prize package of a box at an Ottawa Sens game for 16 of our friends or family. He then asked me if we could go to some more wedding shows together before getting married. We had a great time going to the hockey game and celebrating our upcoming wedding with our families and friends.

On our wedding day, Sylvain went golfing with the guys and I enjoyed a quiet day at my parent's place getting my hair and makeup done with my bridesmaids. Sylvain gave me a beautiful diamond necklace that his sister handed to me with a card expressing his love and excitement for our day. It was a beautiful sunny day in June and perfect weather for our planned outdoor ceremony in the backyard of a local hotel in Cornwall. We were expecting 100 guests, many whom had travelled from out of town.

I was extremely excited to wear my mom's wedding dress and veil after getting some alterations done on it to make it my own and could not wait for Sylvain to see me in it for the first time. We got married at 7 o'clock in the evening on a Saturday night after my dad walked me down the aisle to my grandfather, aunt, uncle and cousin playing soft classical music on their guitars and violins.

The officiant read through our ceremony in both English and French to make sure everyone understood what was being said. As the ceremony went on and Sylvain and I held hands, we stared into each other's eyes, smiled and I knew this was the man I was supposed to spend the rest of my life with.

Our ceremony was followed by a few speeches and then we had our reception right away along with our first dance to the song *I'll Be,* by Edwin McCain.

We took a short honeymoon to the Laurentians since I could only get four days off work and planned to take our "real" honeymoon later that winter. Unfortunately, over the years, our honeymoon kept getting postponed usually for financial reasons, or due to work commitments, or other priorities.

Years later, we finally made plans to take a romantic vacation "honeymoon" for our 15th wedding anniversary, but we only made it to 14 years when he passed away. This is one of my biggest regrets. Take the trip! You never know if you will have tomorrow.

3

THEN COMES THE BABY CARRIAGE

Two years after getting married, we purchased our first home together in the small town of Petrolia in Southern Ontario. We both had good jobs, had paid off our student debts including our wedding expenses, and knew we would be making roots in this town. The house was a bungalow on a quiet cul-de-sac with three bedrooms on the main floor and a finished basement. We were both excited to purchase our first house and create a home where we could start a family. It was the perfect starter home and could be our perfect forever home.

At the age of 25, I was starting to get baby fever. The friends we made in our neighbourhood and from our jobs, all had kids. I loved seeing the kids biking down the street or playing basketball in their driveways and I could not wait for us to start a family.

Sylvain had other ideas. He wanted to billet hockey players. He had a few friends on the Sarnia Police Force that were billet families and we had met some of the kids that lived with them. They were nice and Sylvain wanted to provide a home for teenage boys where they could concentrate on hockey while away from their families. He remembers the families that he used to live with as a teenager when he played hockey and wanted to give back.

After many conversations, and some tears on my end, I talked him out of billeting hockey players - for now - and we decided it was time to try to have a baby. We were shocked to find out we were pregnant after only trying for one month. I felt so excited and started having flashes of our life together with this little person that was going to be made up of part Sylvain and part me. My first thought was who would they look like? Sylvain had dark features - dark brown hair, dark thin shaped brown eyes, long eyelashes, and a big nose, whereas I have blonde hair, blue large round eyes, and a small upper lip. If it is a boy, I really hope they look like him and a girl, I would hope they look like me. It would be so amazing to have little replicas of each of us.

Jacob

I enjoyed being pregnant and the feelings and emotions that came with it. A few weeks into the pregnancy, we had an ultrasound appointment to find out whether we were having a boy or a girl. I do not understand how on earth people can keep this a secret. I have never been good with secrets and we both could not wait to find out the baby's sex. We felt it would be easier to plan on how to decorate the baby's room, whether to buy blue or pink clothes, or what colour stroller we should get.

Sylvain was driving to the hospital for our appointment, and we were both so incredibly excited. We were talking about how we hoped the ultrasound technician would be able to tell the sex and the baby's legs would hopefully not be crossed or anything, but then my cell phone rang.

It was our midwife, and she had some difficult news to share with us. I had previously done some of the normal prenatal tests and one of the tests came back with some alarming results. I put my cell phone on speaker phone so Sylvain could hear too. She continued to explain that our baby had an extremely high probability of being born with spina bifida, which is a condition where the baby's spine and spinal cord do not form properly. She explained that the worst-case scenario would be that the baby's brain does not form properly and there would be a chance of having a stillborn or the best-case scenario was that the baby might have a mild form of it, there won't be any affects whatsoever and they can have a normal life. Somewhere in the middle could mean some surgeries and the possibility of the baby not being able to walk or run.

My heart sank, I started to cry, and Sylvain grabbed my hand. It never even crossed my mind that there was the possibility of complications or health issues. You assume that you will get pregnant and automatically have a normal, healthy baby. Now, finding out the sex of the baby on the way to the hospital did not even matter. The thought of whether the baby was a boy or girl was completely insignificant. We just wanted a healthy baby.

At our ultrasound appointment, we found out we were having a boy. When the ultrasound technician told us, the excitement and joy I thought we would feel in that moment was gone. "Can you tell if the baby has spina bifida?" Sylvain asked. She said it was too early to tell but we would have to go to some follow-up specialty appointments at the London hospital in the next couple of weeks.

The baby was a boy. I was happy that Sylvain would have a son, hopefully a healthy one who he could teach how to skate, and run, and play. The rest of the pregnancy was somber, and the baby's health was always in the back of our mind as a worry.

I had a few strange cravings during my pregnancy such as rice crispy squares and Tim Horton's cream of broccoli soup. Once I even cried in the store when they told me they were out of the broccoli soup, and I had to order another kind of soup. I never made Sylvain run out and get me anything in the middle of the night though. He did however paint my toenails on many occasions when I could not reach anymore, and he made a point when he got home from work to give me a kiss and then get down on a knee and speak French while holding my stomach.

Picking out baby names came with some challenges. We needed to find a name that you could at least pronounce in both French and English, something that was not quite common but not so unique where you had to spell it for everyone. This child would already have to do that with our last name. And a name that would suit a little boy but also a man, something that could be shortened and Sylvain wanted to make sure it would sound good as a hockey nickname. Sylvain's hockey nickname was Roots after our last name - Routhier.

Sylvain leaned towards some French names like Cedric, or Frederique and I liked more common English names that you could at least say in French like Jonathan or Jacob. We decided on the advice from a friend to write the name down on a large piece of paper and post it to the fridge. If we got sick of looking at it or saying it as we walked by, we should try a different name. We agreed on a name, and it stayed on our fridge for the full nine months, so we knew our baby would be named Jacob.

Middle names in both our families were traditionally named after godparents, so we decided to do the same. My brother was the oldest of our three siblings so we decided he would be Jacob's godfather and get his name – James – as a middle name.

I also had a close friend growing up that passed away when we were 18 and I wanted to honour him with using his name as Jacob's middle name as well. So, we decided on Jacob Matthew James Routhier. It had a nice ring to it and could be pronounced in French. He would probably get the nickname Jake as he got older, or Roots like his dad.

My due date came and went, and I honestly thought the baby was never going to come out. Ten days later, my water broke, my contractions started right away, and they were only 30 seconds apart. I could barely catch my breath. This was not the way the midwife explained it would happen. She said they would probably be 5 minutes apart, then 1 minute apart, and then call her, and head to the hospital. Sylvain panicked and drove to the hospital like he was in a police cruiser with lights and sirens on. Thankfully, the streets were empty because it was only 5:30 am.

My labour was quick and easy, and I did it without any drugs or medication. I remember thinking, that was not so bad, I would do that again in a heartbeat. The neat thing with having a midwife was Sylvain could "catch" the baby which is something he was excited to do. The first person to touch our new son as he was being delivered was his dad. He also cut the umbilical cord and placed Jacob on my chest. The midwives then did a thorough check of Jacob and he looked completely fine and healthy, although he was tongue tied. No signs of spina bifida and we were so unbelievably relieved. Sylvain had tears of joy in his eyes, and I remember thinking this was the first time I had ever seen him cry or get emotional.

Nicholas

Adjusting to a new baby came easily to us. We had a

good routine down and Sylvain was extremely helpful. I would get up in the night with the baby, and he would let me sleep in and he would get up early. He would take Jacob in the running stroller and go for jogs, and he would dress Jacob up in his Montreal Canadiens jersey, sit him on his lap and watch hockey games with him. For his first Christmas, he bought him a mini hockey stick and tried to show him how to shoot a ball with it. As soon as he could walk, Sylvain strapped skates to his feet and found a nearby outdoor pond and was trying to get him to skate.

Even though we lived more than 9 hours away from our families, we figured out how to do things on our own. We relied a lot on the close friends we made and paid a lot of money to babysitters over the years. We missed having our parents nearby and used all our vacation time to go back home to visit.

It did not take too long before talk of having another child started. The thought of Jacob having a little brother or sister made me so excited to think about how they would react to each other and play together someday. Sylvain loved being a dad and taking care of a baby, so I did not have to do very much convincing. He did want 6 kids someday because he loved kids so much, but I talked him into let's have one or two and see how it goes first.

We decided to start trying for baby number two not knowing how long it might take. I had friends who had troubles getting pregnant and was worried that it might take us awhile. I was wrong. First month again! I could not believe that we were pregnant already. I felt guilty that it happened so easily for us, yet friends were going through such hard times trying to have a baby.

During my second pregnancy, we opted to not do as much testing as with the first one. We did not want to know ahead of time if the baby was going to have any complications. No matter how the baby turned out, healthy or not, we would love them, and they would be a blessing to our family. We did however want to find out again if it was going to be a boy or girl.

The moment the ultrasound technician told us we were having another boy, I thought how amazing that Jacob would have a brother to become best friends with someday. And then I knew right away, that after this baby, we would have a third. I know you are not supposed to try for a certain sex, but let's face it, I secretly did want a girl at some point.

My second pregnancy went well although I was more tired than the first one. After all, I did have a 1.5-year-old to chase around all the time. And saying Jacob was a busy boy was an understatement! He would not sit still for more than 30 seconds. He was constantly jumping off couches, rolling around on the ground, or taking off down the street. The boys would be 22 months apart and we were in for some busy days ahead.

Sylvain was an incredible husband and helped with anything I needed, whether it was reading or playing with Jacob while I rested, painting my toenails again, giving me back rubs, making dinner, doing the laundry, or cleaning the house. It was easy to have him as a partner to help with raising our kids.

My due date came and went yet again but this baby only made us wait two extra days, thank heavens. My water broke, contractions started, and I called Sylvain at work to let him know it was time. This time my labour was slower, and we did not have to rush so quickly to the hospital. We dropped Jacob off with friends on our way to the hospital and my labour was much more difficult than the first time. I kept remembering my first labour and thought this one would go like clockwork like the previous one. Contractions were more painful and longer, but I was determined to do it completely drug free again. Sylvain was by my side the whole time, holding my hand, placing strands of my blonde hair behind my ear and out of my face, rubbing my back, and reassuring me how much he loved me and could not wait to meet our new son.

The plan was for Sylvain to catch the baby again and when the midwife said: "Ok Sylvain, you can put your gloves on" that is when I knew the moment was close. The baby's head came out but not the rest of him like had happened so easily the first time. The midwife was yelling at me to push, while another one lowered the head of the bed super-fast. I was not sure what was happening because it all happened so fast and seemed a little chaotic. Sylvain asked: "What is going on?" but his question was ignored. The midwives yelled at me again to push as hard as I could and moved Sylvain out of the way and took over trying to deliver the baby. I heard some talk about shoulder dystocia but did not know what that meant at the time. I tried pushing again, was getting extremely exhausted, and with that, the rest of the baby came out. The midwife handed the baby to Sylvain to place on my chest and our son let out a cry.

We decided on the name Nicholas. Even though, we already had a Nicholas in our extended family, that did not matter to us. It was the perfect name for our son. Again, it was easily pronounced in French, he could get the nick-name Nick or Roots, and it went well with Jacob. We gave him the middle name William, which is the English translation for Sylvain's brother's name, who would be his godfather. The enormous sense of responsibility for two little human beings washed over me.

I stayed in the hospital overnight and Sylvain went

home to take care of Jacob. Nicholas was an amazing calm, and easy baby. I think he knew we had our hands full with a very busy 2-year-old so he didn't have a choice but to be a good baby. Nicholas also looked very much like Sylvain, with dark brown hair, big round brown eyes, and he had a massive head. He was also over 9 lbs when he was born and with height in Sylvain's family, we could only assume the boys would be big someday too.

Jacob was really kind with his baby brother. He would help get diapers, hold his bottle for him, push him in the swings, and play peekaboo with him. Nicholas started joining in with watching the hockey games with Sylvain and Jacob, and we had to get a double running stroller so both boys could go on runs with their dad.

Emily

Life was quite busy with two boys however we had many discussions about having a third baby. When would be a good time? Could we handle another one? Were we financially able to make it work? Could we do it with not much help from our families? Would we be ok with 3 boys? What if it was a girl? Life was not made easy for families of 5, booking hotel rooms, or taking an airplane or sitting at a restaurant. We would have to move from man-to-man defense to zone defense.

Because Sylvain was such an incredibly helpful dad to the boys, I knew having another baby with him would not be a problem for us. We decided to have another one because we would be doing this together and I had an amazing partner to help raise our kids.

We planned the timing for baby number 3's arrival so Nicholas would be closer to age 3. Two kids under the age of two was difficult enough, we knew 3 kids under the age of 5 would be even harder and we felt ready. We also did not want the kids to be too far apart in age where they would not grow up together. And we decided to purposely try for a girl. Sylvain did some research on what food to eat, what days were ideal to become fertile, and even what positions were supposed to work.

After our first month of trying, I found out on Christmas day that I was not pregnant. I was completely devastated and could not imagine how people go through the ups and downs of trying to get pregnant, to finding out they are not, month after month. After month two, we found out we were pregnant! We were both so excited and felt so blessed. Our previous concerns about the baby's health continued with this pregnancy but were quickly overshadowed with concerns about my health.

This pregnancy was much more difficult for me and my body was telling me this was it. I had many more complications such as nausea so bad I was on medications, extremely painful sciatica pains to the point I fell a few times throughout my pregnancy, hernia, and a few other issues that I will not go into. I knew after this one, I could not carry another baby and we were satisfied that our family would be complete.

At our ultrasound appointment, we found out we were having girl. I was elated! I could have a little mini-me of my own, with blonde hair and blue eyes, that I could dress up in dresses and play with her hair. I instantly envisioned Sylvain being so gentle with our daughter, surely, she would be daddy's girl and he could dance with her while she is standing on his feet someday, he could twirl her around at her graduation and I could see her dress spin in the air, and he would walk her down the aisle at her wedding. I think I was more excited about seeing how he would be with her than me getting to have a daughter.

It was Thanksgiving weekend and thankfully my brother and his wife were visiting us when I went into labour. They took care of the boys for us while we went to the hospital. If they had not been there, I am not sure who would have watched the boys for us. This was the most difficult part about living far from both our parents.

My labour was much slower this time than for the previous two times. I had time to take a bath before heading to the hospital and once we got to the hospital, we were told to walk for a while and even got some Thanksgiving turkey lunch in the cafeteria. It was not the greatest, at least Sylvain ate.

As my labour progressed, the midwife told me that the baby was turned the wrong way which meant it was probably going to give me a lot of back labour and be more uncomfortable, and boy was she right. The pain was so much worse than what I had experienced in my previous two labours. I had planned on doing it without drugs again but could not take it at one point, and they gave me a type of nitrous gas to help ease the pain. It did help with pain but made my arms and legs go completely numb. I could not move them or lift them up. It was the worst feeling in the world but when the midwife said: "Ok Sylvain, you can put your gloves on", I knew it was almost time.

As she came out, Sylvain placed her on my chest and had to hold her since I could not move my arms. She was crying and had a full head of black hair, and dark brown eyes. More hair than either of the boys had and even though she was the smallest baby I had delivered out of the three, her labour was by far the worst. If I would have had her first, I might not have had any more children after that. So, all three of our kids, looked exactly like their dad with brown hair and brown eyes. They each seemed to get the best features of the both of us as they got older and their personalities started to emerge.

We decided on the name Emily, which was easy to pronounce in French and English, and a middle name of Josee after Sylvain's sister who would be her godmother. It worked out perfectly. We had three kids and three siblings, so each one had a godchild.

Emily was an exceptionally good baby and Sylvain loved to hold her, read her stories, and rock her in the rocking chair. He spoke French to all of them and the boys were also happy to have a baby sister to take care of. Our family of five now felt complete.

4

SYLVAIN'S CAREER

Sylvain knew in high school that he wanted to be a police officer someday. He wanted to be able to help people and make a difference. After graduating from Police Foundations at Algonquin College, Sylvain was quickly hired by the house of commons and worked security at the parliament buildings. This was a great stepping-stone and would give him experience as he applied to Police Forces around Ontario and Quebec.

Sylvain knew the Parliament buildings inside and out, which later came in very handy when an active shooter entered the buildings in 2014.

Sylvain kept applying to police forces and would complain that although he enjoyed his job at Parliament, made a lot of friends, and played on the Parliamentary hockey team, nothing ever happened.

The Ontario Provincial Police was the first to give him an interview, he was ecstatic and at the young age of twenty-four, he started his policing career. His first posting was in Lambton County, which meant a quick move from Ottawa to the Sarnia area after he completed police college. While at the Ontario Police College, he stood out as a leader, won fitness, and leadership awards and I was incredibly proud of him.

The most touching moment for me during his graduation ceremony at the OPP headquarters, was when other officers were handed their badge and a handshake by their father, mother, or family member that was also a police officer. This brought me to tears envisioning Sylvain someday being able to do this if any of our children became police officers someday.

As a young recruit, Sylvain was eager to learn as much as he could from his coach Officer Tim. Tim was a person Sylvain looked up to for many years and they became good friends. Sylvain took overtime shifts, could not wait to come home to tell me about the drunk guy they arrested, or the guy he chased through people's backyards, or how many traffic stops they made. He was excited about the work he was doing and was so happy to be a Police Officer. I was extremely proud of him and elated that he was so happy with his job, until the reality of what could happen set in.

It was a Saturday morning, and I was at work early to run a swim meet. Sylvain was on a night shift the night before and had not come home from work yet when I left, and I thought nothing of it. This was typical of police work. Sometimes they would have to stay later than their shift or often Sylvain had offered to stay and help the other officers with paperwork, so everyone could go home as soon as possible.

The receptionist at my work came and found me to deliver the message that Sylvain called to let me know that if I heard anything on the news, he was ok. My heart sank and I wondered what on earth had happened. I tried calling him back, but he would not answer. I figured he was probably busy dealing with whatever had happened.

When we both got home later that night, he started to recount the story of what happened. Thieves had stolen two vehicles from a nearby city, a police chase started, and they were not far from Sylvain's area. As Sylvain headed towards the area, he heard on his radio that one of the stolen vehicles had rammed into a police cruiser, and then a second cruiser on purpose. Officers had escaped their vehicles, had their guns drawn and were hiding in the ditch. Sylvain came up to one of the stolen vehicles that was flipped over, on fire, and the driver was unconscious on the road. They arrested the other driver, luckily none of the officers were seriously injured. He said the shaky sound of one of his colleague's voices over the radio, while taking cover in the ditch and the fear he heard in her voice, was something he would never forget. As he described what had happened on his night shift, it sounded like a scene out of an action movie, not something that could happen in real life, but now this was our real life.

The possibility of something terrible happening to Sylvain while at work, hit me hard. It was a constant worry every time he left our house and went to work. I often had a hard time sleeping when he was on night shifts. I would play out the scenario in my mind of police officers in white shirts knocking on my door in the middle of the night to tell me Sylvain was injured, and I needed to rush to the hospital. Or worse.

As time went on and he dealt with a lot of difficult things everyday with his job, he stopped getting excited to tell me about every call or scenario. I always asked how his work was, and he would say fine. I never really found out about a lot of the things he dealt with until we were at a work Christmas party or a wedding, and the stories would start to flow. Many times, we would be on our way home from one of these events, and I would feel mad with him because of the story that another officer was telling. Once, another officer told a story about the two teenage girls that were driving home from the bar, crashed their car in a corn field, it caught on fire, and they died. It was the first time I heard about it. Sylvain was there and had to tell their families that they just lost their daughters. I could not understand why he would not have told me about that difficult call when it happened. It brought me feelings of betrayal or like Sylvain could not trust me to tell me what he had been through. I did not figure out until many years later, that he was just trying to protect me.

After being on the road for three years as a regular police officer, Sylvain applied to the OPP's Tactics and Rescue Unit, which is like SWAT that you would see in the movies or tv. Basically, when the OPP dealt with anything really high risk or someone with a weapon, they would call in the Tactics and Rescue Unit (TRU) team.

Sylvain trained his body for months before attending the selection process. 31 candidates started the 10-day tryout, with only 8 finishing and then another 3 getting cut in the months after that. Just getting through the grueling selection process and the 8 months of training that followed, was an incredible accomplishment that not many complete. I was incredibly proud of him and his drive and determination to accomplish something so difficult. This showed Sylvain's character in a lot that he did in his life.

With the TRU team, he started sparing on the West team out of London, and four days after Nicholas was born, he got the call that a permanent opening came up on the

Central Team in Orillia and we would be moving there in 2 months.

While on the TRU team, he would go to work and practice for the big calls, go to the gym, go on training courses, help teach new recruits who were training for TRU, train other police forces on rappelling and was ready to go when duty called. He went on calls about four to five times a week. Most were planned ahead of time and were carried out in the middle of the night, so it didn't affect our family life too much. He went on a lot of high-risk warrants, barricaded calls, K-9 tracks, hostage situations, suicidal cases, and escorting high profile offenders to and from court. He would rappel down buildings, jump out of helicopters, hide in forests so no one could see him, bust down doors, all the things you would see in those action movies. At least, this is what I knew about it. I always had a really hard time believing that this is what he did every day.

At home he was a quiet, calm, and gentle person. He loved to laugh and joke around, especially at his own expense. No matter where we lived or where he worked, he got teased for being French. He had funny expressions he would translate from French into English, or English phrases he would say backwards, like, "I have to pee like a horse race", or "can you put some solar cream on my back?" ("solar cream" meant sunscreen). Rather than becoming self-conscious about his accent, or mistakes in his English, Sylvain used his self-deprecating humour to win people's love and respect.

Sylvain's passions away from work included camping, fishing, golfing, hockey, beer making and tasting, playing practical jokes, dressing up for Halloween and of course his kids and family.

The TRU team job meant we had to schedule our lives

around the possibility of Sylvain getting called out to work at any moment. When a call came, there was no option other than he had to leave immediately and drop whatever we were doing. At times, this meant missing special occasions, Christmases, birthdays, or weddings. Sometimes, it meant having to leave in the middle of dinner at a restaurant. Once, he even left me at a campsite on my own to pack up a tent trailer and two little boys on my own. Anywhere we went, he needed to know how far we were to the closest OPP detachment in case he needed to borrow a car and we always had to have a backup plan.

The hardest part for me was I could never go away, have an overnight somewhere on my own, or visit a friend without being too far away in case he got called for work. Since we did not have our family nearby to help out in these last-minute situations, it took a toll. I felt like I didn't have any freedom, the responsibility of the kids was on me. The only time I could really do anything was when he was on holidays.

Life with two little boys at the time and no family to help became exceedingly difficult. We were still 5 hours away from any family and relying on friends to help us out when needed with the kids. I started to become extremely home sick, exhausted, and resentful. I tried to be the perfect police wife, work full-time, take care of the kids, and be there when Sylvain needed me, but I was running on empty. Sylvain put in his transfer to go to the East Team out of Kingston so we could be closer to family and a few months later, we moved our family again. On the same day in June, we both started our new jobs. Sylvain with the East TRU Team and me as an Aquatics Coordinator for the City of Belleville.

5

SARAH'S CAREER

I always enjoyed swimming as a child, but never realized how much it would affect my life or my career choices. As a child I can remember my dad spending the time playing with my brother and I in my grandparent's pool, letting us jump off his shoulders and teaching us to swim. As we got older, we got our own pool in our backyard and one of the rules in our house growing up was that we had to take swimming lessons each year so we were allowed to swim in our own pool. My dad and grandfather were both lifeguards as teenagers and understood the importance of swimming safely and wanted to instil those values on us. Year after year, I took my swimming lessons and before I knew it, I was only a couple of courses away from becoming a lifeguard and swimming instructor.

BEFORE I WAS FULLY CERTIFIED, I started volunteering as a swimming buddy at our local pool in Cornwall, where I grew up. My role was to help kids with disabilities in regular swimming lessons. I would hold them, assist them, and help integrate them into regular lessons. This was both a difficult job and a rewarding one. It was amazing to see how much the kids improved and progressed from being scared on the side of the pool edge, to swimming around, having fun and being comfortable in the water. At the young age of 14, this was the first time I experienced the true feeling of being able to help other people and feeling like I had a purpose.

I continued my swimming courses and became a certified lifeguard and swimming instructor and had the best part-time job out of all my friends. I spent my summers working at the outdoor pools, being outdoors, enjoying the sun and making sure swimmers were being safe. My dad used to say to me: "You can't be a lifeguard forever; you will need to get a real job someday". Funny enough, most people's real jobs are nowhere near the same amount of responsibility a teenager has when in charge of making sure people do not drown.

I started thinking about what kind of real job I wanted someday. My aunt is a dental hygienist, and this was something that piqued my interest, but I had no idea how hard it would be to just get accepted to school. I got accepted to my second choice of Nursing at Algonquin College in Ottawa, and after graduating high school, I moved to Ottawa.

I spent my first year living in residence learning Nursing and Sylvain at the time was taking Police Foundations at Maisonneuve College in Montreal.

My second year of Nursing school did not go quite as planned. I quickly realized this was not the career for me. The teachers were telling us that all the available jobs when we graduate would be in Nursing homes and I knew I was not cut out to work with seniors. After my first year of school, I got a summer job at the local hospital as a Personal Support Worker working on the Alzheimer's floor and in

Palliative Care. Although, I knew I had a caring personality and wanted to help people, this was really difficult work and I admire people who do this every day.

I DECIDED to quit my Nursing program and take Dental Assisting. It was not the same as being a Dental Hygienist, but at least I could get a job in a Dental office and keep applying to study Hygiene. I worked for a few different Dentists and kept applying year after year to get into the Dental Hygiene program. After 6 years of not being able to get into school for the program I wanted, one day I saw a job advertisement for an Aquatics Coordinator, which would be the person that manages swimming pools, hires, and trains lifeguards and swimming instructors, and creates all the swimming programs. I really missed working at the pool and felt like all that knowledge and skill I learned was no longer being used, and I knew I was going to make another career change.

I QUIT my job as a Dental Assistant and went back to College after Sylvain and I were married. He was incredibly supportive in my decision to change careers. I went to Algonquin and completed my Recreation and Leisure Services Diploma and started redoing all my past swimming certifications and working on some more advanced ones. To manage a swimming pool and get a job as an Aquatics Coordinator, I needed a diploma as well as many advanced qualifications. After I was done my first year of school, Sylvain got the phone call that the OPP had hired him, and we were moving to London so he could attend the Ontario Police College.

. . .

THIS WAS BOTH EXTREMELY exciting and difficult at the same time. I was so happy for Sylvain to get hired by the OPP, but I knew that being far from my family and leaving all our friends would be difficult. It was a sacrifice I was willing to make for my husband and our future, but it was not easy. It meant for the first time, that his career came first and mine would have to be on the backburner. If I could not find the job I wanted, at least I could go back to Dental Assisting if needed.

Luckily, I was able to transfer to Fanshawe College and finish my diploma there while he started working in Lambton County, not far from London. Two weeks after graduating, I got a job as an Aquatics Coordinator for the Town of Petrolia and in six weeks, we were going to be building and opening a brand new indoor aquatic facility.

IT WAS an enormous amount of work to get the pool ready to open. Basically, the water was in the pool and that was it. I had to plan programs and schedules, hire, and train all the staff, purchase safety equipment, uniforms, and pool toys, and develop policy and procedures. I worked many hours and when we opened, the facility and staff were ready to go. This was a relatively small pool with one 4 lane 25-metre pool and a therapeutic pool, and it was a great job for me to learn the ins and outs of managing a pool and staff.

FANSHAWE COLLEGE CONTACTED me shortly after the pool opened asking if I would be willing to teach in the Recreation and Leisure Services program. I was honoured to be given the opportunity and spent one day a week driving the hour and half to London to teach students and offer my experience managing a recreation facility. After Jacob was born, I took a break from teaching so I would have more time to devote as a mom but knew I would want to teach again someday.

When Sylvain's job took us to Orillia after being in Lambton County for 4 years, I was happy to be on maternity leave when Nicholas was born and did not have the pressure of needing to find a job right away. Aquatic Coordinator jobs are few and far between with usually only one job per city. It was hard to leave my job and friends we had made and relied on and start fresh in a new city, but I knew that was what was best for our family.

Once my maternity leave was over, I was extremely fortunate to get a job as an Aquatics Coordinator for the City of Barrie. I oversaw running one of three pools operated by the city. I went from having a staff of 15 in Petrolia, to now a staff of 50 and working in an extremely fast-paced environment. I quickly learned how complex it was to manage people, how to deal with customer complaints, how to be highly creative in maximizing program space, and what it meant to work in a large team. I was also approached to teach again at the college level at Georgian College in the Ski and Snowboard Operator Program, although I had never skied a day in my life!

A few years later, we felt that Orillia was still too far from home and our families and made the move to Kingston when the OPP TRU team had an opening there for Sylvain. I could not believe my luck when I got a job as an Aquatics Coordinator for the City of Belleville, only 45 minutes from Kingston, and we would be opening a brand new exceptionally large aquatics Centre. This job was perfect for me! It was a larger operation than Petrolia but not as large as Barrie. Again, I went to work planning, organizing, and getting ready for everything to open. The new facility opened and a month later, Emily was born, and I went on maternity leave.

Trying to balance both our careers, kids, activities, friends, and family was not easy. Sylvain's job came first, our kids came next, then my job and so on. I was lucky that I was able to schedule some of my work hours that were required in the evenings and weekends when Sylvain was off, but this meant we did not get to see each other very often. We relied on daycares and babysitters since we still did not have any family nearby. I used to always wonder how single parents made it work and that no matter whatever happened in our marriage, I would never want to be a single parent.

I LOVED my job because it gave me a sense of purpose other than being a mom. I felt I had accomplished a lot and was proud of where I had made it in my career. I thought I would stay in my job forever and loved the people I worked with and the work I did, and I was good at it! Do not get me wrong, I also loved being a mom. I loved holding our kids when they were babies, I loved rocking them at night and singing to them. I enjoyed watching them grow into their own little people, developing their own personalities, and needing me. Our family was perfect.

When I came back from maternity leave, I was excited to

get back to my job but also accepted a volunteer position with the Canadian Red Cross as a Water Safety Ambassador. This position would allow me to attend Aquatic Conferences, network with other Aquatic Coordinators, be an advocate for the water safety programs offered by the Canadian Red Cross and create and deliver sessions at the conferences based on drowning prevention. I became extremely comfortable speaking to large audiences about topics that were important to me. I knew that by sharing what I had learned in the industry, others could implement tools at their own pools to help prevent drownings. Again, helping other people became a focus and something I felt very strongly about doing. I feel that this volunteer position was instrumental in preparing me for what was coming.

6

HOCKEY LIFE

Hockey was always a vital part of Sylvain's life as a player, a fan, a coach, and a billet parent. He loved the game and he loved that it taught team-work, discipline, and determination. He enjoyed being an athlete, playing in tournaments, how it brought together friendship, competition and wearing his favourite team's jersey whenever he could – the Montreal Canadiens.

I AM NOT sure what we were thinking. I thought that having our own three kids was enough to juggle, but we also decided to start billeting hockey players - something Sylvain was very adamant about since he had that experience at a young age. He wanted to provide young hockey players who were away from home, a comfortable place to stay so they could concentrate on their hockey careers.

Sylvain grew up playing a high level of hockey, as did his brother and sister. I do not know how his parents managed juggling three kids playing travel hockey, but they did it. At

the age of 15, Sylvain was drafted to the Chicoutimi Sague-
neens in the Quebec Major Junior Hockey League but
decided to move to Ontario and try his hockey skills there.
His goal was to get a university scholarship in the United
States for hockey and learn how to speak English.

Leaving home at the age of 15 to a new city and getting
bumped around to different billet families depending on
which hockey team he was playing for, was hard on him.
Some houses he lived in were tough on him with lots of
rules in place, but others treated him like their own son and
created a loving family atmosphere that he appreciated for
many years.

OVER THE NEXT couple of years, he played hockey for the
Pembroke Lumber Kings, the Nepean Raiders, the Alexan-
dria Glens, the Kemptville 67's and the Akwesasne Wolves.

Sylvain started talking about wanting to billet hockey
players when we first moved to Sarnia and some police
friends of his were billeting some of the Sarnia Sting players. We did not even have kids of our own yet, but he wanted
to have teenage boys live with us so he could give them a
great billet experience. I managed to post-pone his billeting
ideas until one day I met two hockey players when we were
living in Belleville at Subway.

I was standing behind them and I could tell by their size
and stature that they must have been players for the Ontario
Hockey League's Belleville Bulls. I started a conversation
with them, asking how their billet families were. They were
both polite, very well-spoken young men and I could not
wait to tell Sylvain about the experience and that I was
ready to billet hockey players if he wanted to do it.

. . .

AFTER TALKING about the idea for a few days and figuring out the logistics and how we would handle it, we contacted the team and went through the interview process to be a billet family. We had a spare bedroom and bathroom in our basement, with a finished living room and a mini stick hockey rink. Sylvain had painted red and blue lines on the basement concrete, along with boards all the way around, and mini stick nets. It was a perfect setup for a young hockey player.

It was October and the season had already started so all the players already had homes however the team had just made a trade and a new player was moving to Belleville from London and would need a place to stay.

Brett moved in with us and at first kept to himself but eventually he easily became a part of our family. He would play mini sticks with the boys and let Emily play with his hair. We attended all his home games as a family and would listen to the away games on the radio. His parents were unbelievably kind to us, and our kids and it was clear they were thankful that their son did not have to worry about his home life and could concentrate on his hockey career. The highlight of our weeks was going to watch him play hockey and he was really good. It was like the boys had a big brother that was a pro hockey player and he lived with us. They would wear Brett's hockey jersey, that his parents bought for them, with his last name on their backs to all the games. Jacob would copy how Brett did his hair and loved it when he had some of his hockey buddies over to play mini sticks with them. Often, we would have another player or two stay for dinner, and I enjoyed having a house filled with teenagers and lots of hockey talk. I think Sylvain felt like he was back part of the team in some way. It would bring back many memories of his days hanging with his hockey buddies, talking about their games, and he would forget that he was the adult in the house.

As the hockey season came to an end, our city received shocking news that the team had been sold and would not return for another season. This news rocked the City of Belleville, the players, the employees, and our family. This meant we would not be able to billet again. Brett was over-aged and was planning on playing hockey in university so we knew he would not be coming back. We had just done one season of billeting and already the kids were talking about getting another player next year, and we knew that would not happen.

The day Brett moved out and went back to his family in London, was especially hard on both Sylvain and me. We both cried as we hugged Brett and said our goodbyes, not knowing where we would see him again. It felt like our little brother was moving away and we both knew that he would move on and probably forget about us and the kids.

We took a year off from billeting as the city tried to figure out how to replace the hockey team. We felt like there was a void in our family with not having the hockey games to go to and the hustle and bustle of teenage hockey players around the house.

The following year, there was still no hockey team and one day while I was at work, I got a phone call from the front desk saying that there was a family here to speak with me. I did not know them but as I approached and asked how

I could help, the dad introduced me to his wife and their son, Brendan. They drove here from about four hours away and were desperate to find a billet home for their son who was a goalie for the Picton Pirates. They thought they would come to the wellness centre, where I worked and where there were four ice rinks and would ask around if anyone knew of billet families. The team had run out of billet families and Brendan was sleeping on a friend's couch that was housing three other players too. My heart went out to this family, and I could hear and see the desperation for these parents to know that their son was in a safe place while they were far away.

Brendan moved in a week later and again we opened our home and our family to this young man. He instantly bonded with the kids and would be the goalie for many mini stick games. He enjoyed playing with the kids and would often offer to babysit so Sylvain and I could have a dinner night out. Picton was further away for us to go and see his hockey games and by now, the boys were also playing travel hockey and our schedule did not allow us to catch as many of his games.

Having teenage boys to feed and clean up after was not as difficult as I originally thought it would be. Yes, they did eat a lot, but I was already making meals for five people, so one more adult was not much of an inconvenience. They would give me grocery lists to make sure we had all their favourite foods stocked up and I learned some of their favourite mom's recipes to cook for them.

The rule in our house was it was up to them to keep their room clean, and they oversaw cleaning their own bathroom as well as doing their own laundry. It was easy having Brett and Brendan live with us. We trusted them both with our kids and having a daughter in the house was not a worry since she was under the age of four. There is no way we were going to billet hockey players once she was a teenager! Sylvain also enjoyed having them around, watching hockey games with them, and getting help with maintaining the outdoor rink.

YES, we had an outdoor ice rink in our own backyard. Sylvain started building the rink as soon as Jacob was able to start skating. At first, it was just a small ice rink with some short boards around the sides. Over the years, it grew to a whopping 55 feet x 35 feet rink. It was massive and it had lights for night playing, full boards all the way around, benches, and even a make-shift Zamboni. He was handy and made the boards himself. Just setting up the boards and taking them down to store was an enormous task. The years we had Brett and Brendan living with us, made setting up the rink and taking it down easier since some teenage elbow grease came in handy.

EACH YEAR, he would research what else he could build to add onto the rink to make it bigger or better. He watched endless videos on how to paint the boards, how to get the ice smooth, when was the perfect time to fill it with water, and more. He spent many hours watering the rink, patching holes, setting up drills for the kids, and strapping on his skates or some old goalie equipment to practice outside with them. It became a passion, an obsession, and a way to teach his kids about the sport he loved.

Each winter, we would invite the kid's whole hockey teams over for a skate, potluck, and bonfire. It took some careful planning to make sure the weather would cooperate, the kids travel hockey schedules would work, and Sylvain's was off work. It was the talk of the teams, year after year as it was an event, we all looked forward to. The kids would spend hours outside skating, and I always had hot chocolate ready for when they came in with rosy cheeks and had enough.

7

POLICE CAREER CHANGES

S ylvain really enjoyed working on the East TRU team and he used to brag that he had the best job in the whole OPP organization. He made some great connections with guys on the team and so did I with many of the wives. We were part of a club that not many belonged to. Not many people could understand what it was like to support an officer who dealt with high-risk crazy stuff and the crazy schedule that went with it. The guys would go to the gym everyday together, we would socialize as families, celebrate birthdays, anniversaries, and graduations together. It was a brotherhood of men for Sylvain, and a community for our whole family. The officers would play pranks on each other, surely to lighten the mood and the work they had to deal with.

He had to go away a lot for training, teaching other officers his craft of rappelling, and it was no doubt hard on me being alone while he was away to raise our three young kids.

In March of 2016, after seven years on TRU, Sylvain made the very emotionally difficult decision to leave the team and go back to the road as a regular police officer. The

TRU team had a few going away parties for him and Sylvain's Staff Sergeant tried to convince him to change his mind many times. They did not want him to leave but Sylvain had different career aspirations.

All three of our kids were playing a lot of hockey and he was coaching all of them. The boys were playing AA and traveling a lot and he was finding it very hard to be at all their games with getting called out. It was very difficult to balance work and home life.

Going back to the road as a regular police officer in a new detachment, was easy for Sylvain. He quickly learned the ropes again and many of his colleagues looked up to him from his experience on the TRU team and dealing with high-risk situations. He had lots to share and would often tell the funny or interesting stories that he encountered as a TRU member.

One in particular, happened in 2014 when an active shooter entered the Parliament buildings in Ottawa. His TRU team got called to attend as backup for the Ottawa tactical team, who were clearing the buildings to make sure there were no more shooters. Sylvain's previous knowledge of the Parliament buildings from working there many years earlier came in quite handy that day.

Working the road was different this time around for Sylvain. He seemed to have a harder time dealing with the regular calls and the emotional toll it put on him. He especially had a much harder time with calls that involved children, since this time around being a dad gave him a different perspective.

I remember one call that he had to investigate where a 4-year-old girl had been sexually assaulted over a two-year period. Sylvain had to explain to her parents how this had happened, to what extent it happened, and that the person who had been doing this to their daughter was someone they knew. I knew this had hit Sylvain hard because our daughter was also a 4-year-old at the time. I knew Sylvain immediately thought about how this child could have been our daughter and as he started to tell me more about the case, he stopped and said: "I can't tell you anymore, it is too awful, and I don't want this to bother you and for you to have nightmares." I was thankful that he wanted to spare me the details. I remember wondering; what else has he seen at work that he has not told me about because he wants to protect me?

He did tell me about general calls he went to. Many car accidents and deaths, having to do death notifications, domestic disputes including one that lead to a death, and many suicide calls. He had seen people get hit by trains, people who had hung themselves, shot themselves, and died by carbon monoxide in their car. In some ways, being on the road was more dangerous and more difficult than when he was on the TRU team.

After about two years of being on the road, Sylvain started talking to me about wanting to become a Sergeant. He felt like it was the next step for him in his career and that he had a lot to offer as a leader. He wanted to become a road Sergeant first since there was often job postings and the opportunities would be available, and then someday return to the TRU team as a Sergeant.

I felt proud of him wanting to make this next step and supported him through the process. He applied for three Sergeant jobs all at detachments close to where we lived so we would not have to move our family. He studied for months, took psychological tests, talked to other Sergeants and Staff Sergeants who were friends to get advice, and had to prepare essays and presentations. He knew getting one of the three spots would not be easy since he did not have any "Acting" time under his belt like many of the other applicants. In total 18 people applied for the jobs and the anticipation leading up to finding out if he was successful or not, was excruciating. I had prepared myself to support him and be positive if he did not get a position. Surely, he would be so disappointed but at least, he knew what the process was and had the experience of interviewing for the next time.

The phone call came when we were both in the kitchen preparing dinner one evening before Christmas. The kids were downstairs playing and as Sylvain answered the phone, I could see the nervousness in his eyes. I could also hear the woman's voice through the phone say, "Congratulations Sylvain, you got the Sergeant job at the Quinte West Detachment!"

Sylvain's eyes almost bugged out of his head, his mouth and jaw dropped to the ground. He was trying to contain his excitement as he thanked her and listened for details. I started crying feeling so happy for him and so proud. He got off the phone and literally started jumping up and down like a small child on Christmas morning. He kept repeating: "Holy smokes, I can't believe it! How is this possible? Oh, my goodness! Honey, I'm going to be a Sergeant!" We hugged repeatedly as I let him bask in his excitement and he started to call his parents to tell them the good news.

Sylvain became a Sergeant in January of 2018. He found the transition to this new role very difficult, with little to no training. He was very hard on himself and wanted to be the best Sergeant. He would go on the road and help with the calls when the call volumes rose, he would help mentor the other officers, and was the person everyone went to with their problems or concerns. Managing people was hard for him but he thought back to all the previous, amazing

Sergeants he had during his 13 years as a police officer and remembered what made them great. He tried to mimic those qualities. As a Sergeant, he also had to deal with some difficult calls but this time, he had to lead his team.

Three months into his new job, he didn't come home on time from his day shift. He called and mentioned they were dealing with a sudden death, and he might get home before I went to bed. Around 10:30 that night, he came home, took a shower, and crawled into bed. I asked him if everything was ok. He said they had a sad call where a 37-year-old woman who was living in a group home had passed away. The staff were taking it really hard since they were like her family, and everyone was crying. We were both also 37 years old at the time. As he looked at me, I could tell the thought ran through his mind, that 37 would be way too young for anyone to pass away. I asked him if he was ok again. He said yes, he was fine, and we fell asleep.

The next day, April 14th, 2018, after another long day shift, he came home, walked in the front door, and started crying.

In nineteen years of being with him, I think I had only seen him cry twice before, both times at family funerals. I was shocked and asked him what was wrong. He started telling me he thought something was wrong with him. People at work were asking him questions and he had to keep asking them to repeat themselves. He could not concentrate or focus on anything. He then told me he had not slept in a week because he couldn't turn off his mind. He wasn't sleeping, working twelve-hour shifts, running around with kids' activities, hockey, working out and trying to carry on so no one would notice.

That night, I was cleaning up after dinner, getting the kids ready for bed and went to check on him in our room.

He was having a hard time forming sentences and I initially thought maybe he was having a stroke. He couldn't stop crying and started questioning things such as "why are we on this earth?", and "what is our purpose?" It scared me to see him in such a confused state and I couldn't figure out what had happened. He was shaken up by the sudden death of that thirty-seven-year-old woman the previous day. Over the years, he had told me about many difficult calls, but never once, was I ever worried about him. This time it was different.

Normally, he would brush things off like it was fine or like he was fine. He was such an easygoing person, and nothing ever bothered him. Or at least, he hid it from me and everyone else very well.

The next morning, he told me that he still couldn't sleep and couldn't turn off his brain, although he wouldn't elaborate.

"I can run out to the drug store and get you some sleeping pills, you just need to get some sleep", I offered, not thinking anything drastic about it.

When he responded with, "I don't think you can leave me alone right now."

I was very confused by his response.

"Honey, are you having thoughts of hurting yourself?", I asked tentatively.

He said, "Yes, and I think you need to take me to the hospital."

I was completely shocked and silently scared. I began to make the arrangements so we could go to the hospital. It was the worst day in the world to drive anywhere! It had been freezing rain for almost 24 hours straight and a layer of ice covered everything outside. I asked him if he wanted me to call in sick for him since clearly, he was not going to be able to go to work today. He said no, he had already called.

I called my brother and asked if I could drop off the kids. I didn't want to tell him too many details but just said that something is wrong with Sylvain and I need to bring him to Emerg. He could not believe we were going to try to drive anywhere in the ice storm since we lived out in the country but I needed someone to watch the kids so Sylvain and I could go figure out what was going on.

I could not believe what was going on. I told the kids that "daddy's head hurt" and I needed to take him to the hospital and we were going to bring them to their aunt and uncle's house to play.

I drove because Sylvain was not in the proper mindset to do so. After I dropped the kids off, I held his hand while tears slowly ran down his face. I squeeze his hand gently and told him that it would be ok and that we will get help.

8

SUICIDE TALK

We sat outside of the hospital entrance, in our vehicle for forty-five minutes while I tried to convince him to just walk in the doors with me. He did not want to go in. He had been there many times bringing people to the emergency department. He knew the staff there and was so ashamed that he himself needed help.

He said to me, before we go in, there is something you need to know because it will probably come out while we are in there. I was scared. What was he about to tell me? He cried some more as he worked up the nerve to talk to me.

Finally, he went into the hospital.

He met with a crisis intervention worker for about two hours. I wasn't allowed in the room with him because as Sylvain started to talk, the councillor looked at me and said maybe it's best if you step out for a moment. I sat in the hall, scared, confused, not knowing what to do. The doctor discussed admitting him however decided to send him home with me with a prescription for an anti-anxiety medication and a sleep medication.

I took the week off work to be with him and to try to

figure out what was going on. He called his staff sergeant to tell him he was going through some stuff and needed time off work. His boss was more than supportive, didn't ask questions and encouraged him to take the time he needed to get better. He tried calling the Employee Assistance Program (EAP) through his work asking to see a counsellor. They set up a telephone appointment for him the following week, but he decided to cancel it since the hospital had set him up with an in-person meeting with a psychologist in three days. I went with him to that meeting and when they called his name, I stood up to go with him, but they told me it was just him they wanted to see, so I waited in the waiting room.

We left that appointment with a doctor's note to be off work. On the drive home, I asked Sylvain what she told him, but he couldn't remember much from the conversation. When we got home, I called the office to see if I could meet with the doctor and ask some questions. She couldn't tell me any details of what they discussed due to doctor-patient confidentiality agreements. I asked questions to clarify specifics to do with his medications, things like - should he drive? What are the side effects of the medication? What is the diagnosis? She told me he had anxiety and a sleep disorder. He would continue to see her and a counsellor through the hospital on a weekly basis.

Looking back now, I wish I would have pushed this issue further. If my husband had a brain tumour, I would have been allowed in all his appointments with him. I would have known what he was telling his doctors about his symptoms. I would have known exactly what the treatment plan was. I would have known what signs and symptoms to look for if his situation got worst. I knew him better than anyone else. I wish I would have been able to tell his doctor when I noticed changes in him. This is an illness that someone cannot go through alone and the support of closest family members or friends is imperative. I found out after he passed away that he could have signed a consent form to allow me in his appointments with him. I wish I had known about that before it was too late.

LATER THAT WEEK, Sylvain and I had a very difficult conversation. I finally asked him, if he had a suicide plan when he was having thoughts of hurting himself. It was hard to even say the word suicide and I did not want to be so direct. The word suicide made my stomach turn. I could not believe this was a conversation I needed to have with him. I felt that I needed to know but feared the answer he was going to give me.

So, instead I worded it: "are you having thoughts of hurting yourself?" and "Did you have a plan to end your life?" He told me he did. What? I could not believe what came out of his mouth. He drove to work on the Friday morning in a rage and was hoping that someone would hit him, and he would get into a car accident. My stomach dropped thinking about how he could have easily hurt or killed someone else while trying to do this. I could not believe that he woke up that morning so upset and angry over something and he tried to die. I would have been at a complete loss and would have been completely blindsided not knowing anything that was going on with him. If he would have been in his police cruiser, he would have died in the line of duty and there would have been a lot of honour that would have come with his passing.

When nothing happened, because it was five in the morning and no one else was on the roads, his plan was to go to work on Sunday and shoot himself with his gun. The thought and vision of him doing this crushed my heart to the point of unexplainable pain. I felt nauseous just thinking about it and a quick visual flashed through my mind that involved blood and his limp body. How on earth could he be thinking about doing this? How was he making these plans to end his life and I did not even know? So many thoughts were rushing through my head. I felt so betrayed that he would have kept this all a secret from me when I was here and made a promise to always be by his side and help him through anything. Thank heavens he did not go through with it. Oh my goodness, how devastating this would have been on our parents....our kids? How would our friends react? His coworkers? His siblings? My siblings? How would I explain what had happened? I wanted to break down screaming and crying in front of him and beg him to not think that way again. To promise to me to never think that way again or to make plans to leave me and our kids. What the heck was going through his head that this was an option he was considering? Would me simply telling him that he could not do that be enough to stop him? Who is this person? What had happened to the man I love?

I never knew anyone who died by suicide. I only heard about people who had attempts or were successful and Sylvain had to attend as a police officer. Sylvain would sometimes tell me the details around how they died but I never really knew the backstory. I never knew about the people who cared about that individual or if they were suffering from a mental illness or not.

Sylvain had an uncle that jumped in front of a subway in Montreal and died because of financial issues but that was before he was born. His family never really discussed his uncle or how it affected anyone or what would make a person get to that point. I only ever thought that people who committed suicide must have been in a real bad place and hated their lives so much that they did not want to live anymore. It was something that happened to other people, not to people I knew.

Sunday was the day he told me he was having suicidal thoughts and I took him to the hospital instead. I asked him what made him stop from following through with his plan. I was trying to understand his world and what he was thinking and going through. It was really difficult for me to understand any of it. He told me he couldn't bear the thought of inconveniencing anyone else. Someone from work would have found him and someone would have had to clean up a mess. What? I thought. Wait a minute. He didn't commit suicide because he was worried about another first responder having to see him? That was it? It wasn't the thought of leaving his kids or putting me or our family through hell? It wasn't the thought that he would miss watching our kids grow up? Graduations? Weddings? Special family moments or vacations? This did not make any sense to me. Did he not care about the kids or about me enough for that to make him stop from taking his own life? I was so confused and tried not to get angry. I thought I was going to throw up. I could tell he was in a fragile state. He must have thought about all the times he had to see a dead body from someone who killed themselves and did not want to put his co-workers through that. Even when trying to plan his own death, he was thinking about his coworkers. It hurt that he wasn't thinking about his family, his kids, or me. But thank God he did not go through with it and he asked for help. I felt a huge amount of relief that we had gotten over that hurdle. Suicide was no longer an option for him, and we were working on getting him the help he needed instead.

Over the next couple of months, we talked often about suicide and how devastating it would be on our kids and family and how there were other options. He promised me that if he was ever having such thoughts again, he would talk to me about it. He wasn't a child. He was a grown man and I trusted him.

I asked him often if he was having thoughts of hurting himself and whenever I did, he always responded with some version of, "Don't worry honey, I would never do that. It was in the past and I know now to get help."

I wanted to believe him.

CHANGES

Over the next couple of weeks that followed, I saw major changes in Sylvain. He no longer smiled, laughed, or joked around. He didn't want to be in social settings. He had a hard time remembering anything or concentrating. We took things day by day, being careful to try to carry on like everything was normal around our kids.

Sylvain was still having a hard time sleeping and was diagnosed with Tinnitus. He had a constant ringing or sloshing sound in his ear that was worse at night when he was trying to sleep. He eventually told me that this had started about two months prior to him going off work. Perhaps a physical symptom of stress that he tried to ignore? Or a symptom from years of shooting guns?

All Sylvain could talk about everyday was wanting to go back to work. He felt such a huge amount of guilt for being off work since he just got a new job as a Sergeant and was leaving his shift short. He convinced his doctor to sign him off to go back to work in mid-May. I believe he told his doctor anything she needed to hear to sign him off. His use of force was taken away, even though I hadn't told anyone what his suicide plan had been, and he was put on desk duties.

His doctor relayed the information about his return-to-work plan through paperwork to his supervisor that he could return to work on light duties, but not go on calls or have the use of a firearm.

He cried driving home from work every single day. He felt useless and completely incompetent and felt that they were just trying to find him work to fill his days with. He would see his coworkers leaving on calls in their cruisers and he could hear the calls come in through the radios. He felt so ashamed that he wasn't allowed to go with them. He was good enough to get a job as a Sergeant but now, only a few months later, he could not even do the job of a normal police officer. Stripping a police officer of their use of force has such a larger meaning and symbolism than I could possibly ever understand. However, I saw it through Sylvain's eyes. For 13 years, being a police officer was Sylvain's existence and being a husband and father came secondary. Being a police officer was something he was so proud of, and it came with prestige in anything we both did. People respected him because of his job, and thought very highly of him, but suddenly that was all taken away from him. It was demoralizing and I could understand where the shame came from.

Sylvain once told me that he was the first person to judge other officers that always called in sick or were off work for long periods of time because he didn't understand. But now he got it. After a week and a half, he went off work again realizing that he wasn't getting better and being at work was causing more stress.

He decided to quit drinking alcohol and coffee to try to

be able to think more clearly. He started not wanting to get out of bed, not eating as much, and no longer working out. He kept his emotions in all day until the kids went to bed and then cried every night. He was also diagnosed with depression after I recognized the signs. He seemed sad all the time, wasn't doing things he normally wanted to such as working out or even taking a shower. I looked up a question-naire online and asked him questions. The results said he had depression and I suggested he talk to his doctor about this the next time he saw her. Sure enough, she added depression to his diagnosis and gave him more medication. I looked up all the medications he was on to familiarize myself with them and I was concerned about one in particu-lar. As I was reading the side effects, it said one of the side effects could be suicidal ideation. I told Sylvain about this and ask him if he thought this medication was a good idea or not? He said if the doctor has prescribed it, then we should trust that she knows what she is doing.

About a year prior to all this happening with Sylvain, I took the Psychological First Aid course with the Canadian Red Cross. I wanted to take the course so I could learn more about how to help my aquatic staff who struggle with mental illness. I felt like handing them an Employee Assistance Program brochure didn't seem like enough. Never did I think I would be taking what I learned and applying it to my personal life.

I started noticing more changes in Sylvain. It was like he was walking around in a fog all the time. I could see his mind was always racing and he had a hard time being present in the moment with us. He started to tell me that work calls were starting to bother him. Calls he had been on ten years ago that he never thought about before were starting to surface. I told him to talk to his doctor about these thoughts. I was starting to suspect that he could have PTSD, post-traumatic stress disorder. I remembered times he had nightmares, but I thought PTSD was only for people who had gone to war. I started doing some of my own research and was convinced this was what was going on with Sylvain. After his next doctor's appointment, I asked him if she had diagnosed him with PTSD yet. He said no, they will probably get to that at his next appointment. Later, after reading through his medical records, he never told his doctor any of this which is why he was never officially diagnosed with PTSD.

He started developing a severe temper with our kids. Something that was completely out of character for him. He would snap at them for the simplest things.

Every summer we went on an annual camping trip with all of my extended family to a campground I grew up going to. It was the place I had all the best childhood memories from swimming, canoeing, cliff jumping, fishing, campfires, and being with family. We wanted our kids to grow up having those memories as well. We took the kids for the week to Charleston Lake, hoping that some time away would help us navigate what Sylvain was going through. It was the first time my parents saw him since he had been off work, and they could tell he was not himself. It was a stress-free, relaxing week, spending time in nature, without the distractions of our busy lives and I thought it would help.

We had an annual ritual at Charleston Lake where one evening when the sun was setting, we would all walk down to the beach, watch the sunset, and each family would take a turn standing at the waters edge, facing the sunset, and we would get family pictures done. The resulting photos from each year and seeing how much the kids grew, and the effect of the black outline of our family in front of the beautiful sunset was breathtaking. I did not know at the time that this would be our last family photo of the five of us all together.

After a few weeks, Sylvain's temper quickly turned to what I would describe as severe paranoia. He kept telling me that he thought he was going to lose his job. He thought the OPP was going to hire a private investigator to investigate him. He felt he had falsified his application to become a sergeant, they wrongfully chose him, and they were going to find out that he copied answers from someone else during the interview process. I knew for a fact that he didn't copy anything because I proofread all his answers and had to fix all his French grammar!

His delusions and paranoia were even spilling into our home life. He thought we wouldn't have money to pay for kids hockey this year and we would eventually lose our house.

No matter how much I reassured him that everything he was believing wouldn't happen, he didn't believe anything I said to him. I finally convinced him to setup a meeting with his staff sergeant. I just needed him to tell Sylvain that all his worrying was not necessary, that he didn't cheat on anything, and he wouldn't lose his job for being off work. The weekend before his meeting with his boss, he started having anxiety attacks about the meeting.

On Monday, July 23rd, eight days before he passed, we went to his police detachment for his meeting. We met with his boss for about two hours. Sylvain's boss told him everything I needed him to hear. It was perfect! He told Sylvain why they chose him as a sergeant. It was because of the person he was and how he treated other people. Plus, his boss explained, Sylvain had excelled in the interview process and had impressed the interview committee and scored as the top candidate. The boss continued to appease

Sylvain, assuring him that his shift would be fine, and he needed to take time off to get himself better.

This meeting should have squashed all his paranoia thoughts about his job. Yet, as we drove home, he was very quiet. I asked him how he thought the meeting went and he said, "I think we need to sell our trailer."

I was shocked. He was worried about our finances and went on and on about why we should sell. This broke my heart. I didn't want to sell our trailer and it seemed the paranoia went from his job right to something else right away.

Later that day, Sylvain's Staff Sergeant called us to ask us to go back into the office to fill a WSIB claim form. He felt the stress Sylvain was feeling was a cause of many years of accumulating stress and moving to a new detachment and starting a new job caused that level of stress to overflow. I agreed, he was right. I started thinking that maybe it was time to try changing his medication. Sylvain was still crying everyday even though he was on an anti-depressant, he was having anxiety attacks even though he was on an anti-anxiety medication and he still was having a very hard time sleeping even though he was on sleep medications.

On Wed, July 25th, he called his doctor to see if he could get an appointment to change his meds. They gave him an appointment for August 8th, over two weeks away. This was not good enough for me. I called the office myself and left a message saying that I was very concerned about my husband, and I would really appreciate it if they could see him right away. He went to the hospital later that day and left with a new anti-anxiety medication to try. Two days later, his doctor agreed to let him go back to work and was working on his "return-to-work" paperwork.

After a couple of days on this new medication, we went to our trailer for the weekend and it was like for the first time since all this started back in April, I had the old Sylvain was back!

He was laughing and smiling again, joking around, had lots of energy, came to campfires, and started fixing everything that was broken around the trailer.

We got home that Sunday night and I remember telling him, "Wow, do you realize you just had two really great days of no crying?"

I thought to myself, "Finally, this is amazing! this medication is going to help him get better!"

That was two days before he died.

The coroner later told me that sometimes this is a sign that someone has made up their mind, and all the stress has been lifted all their shoulders and they have made peace with their decision.

10

THE AFTERMATH

I started researching treatment centre options for depression, anxiety, for First Responders, but I couldn't find anything. I thought Sylvain just needed to get away from our busy everyday life, maybe meet other people going through something similar, and concentrate on himself so he could get better. He needed some peer support and to realize that recovery from a mental illness is possible. All my searches came up with addiction-based centres or were in the United States and would be very expensive. Sylvain hadn't turned to drugs or alcohol to cope with what he was going through.

That's why I knew, from the moment I got to our house and his car was not in our driveway.

For a moment, I thought about going to wait for him at my brother's house, but something propelled me to go into the house and look around. I walked into our bedroom and on our bed was a handwritten note. I knew exactly what it was as soon as I saw it.

He left me a suicide note.

I couldn't read it at first, I just skimmed it quickly until I saw the line "if the police are looking for me, this is where I am."

He named his location which was not far from our house.

I frantically called 911 and told them my husband just left me a suicide note. I told them his location and as the dispatcher arranged to send the police and paramedics to his location. I had a moment to read the entire note.

Part of it read;

"Sarah, what I have done is unthinkable and I don't deserve to be around anymore… I can't spend any more time with you and the kids realizing what I have done to you and I know you will never forgive me. Please tell my family I'm sorry. The police can find me in a lane off of Bronk Rd north of Harmony Rd.

Sylvain"

The dispatcher asked me to read her the letter a couple of times to make sure she got all the correct information. I was having a hard time to compose myself and stop crying long enough to get the words out. His words. Possibly his last words to me ever. And this is what he wants to say? Oddly enough, I did really care in that moment about anything that he wrote in the letter. I just wanted him to be alive. Please, be alive. Please, let it not be too late.

I told the dispatcher; "I think I should tell you that he is an OPP Sergeant."

She paused before asking, "What's his name?"

I told her his name. She paused again and said, "I'm so sorry, I know your husband well. I hear him on the radio all the time and I've met him at the communication centre. Don't worry, we're all family and we're going to find him."

She said give me a few minutes, as she explained that she arranged for two officers to come and wait with me at the house. She told me their names and they were his TRU boss and his very close TRU friend.

As she was making the arrangements, I texted Sylvain's sister in Montreal to let her know I found a suicide note and the police were trying to find him. I asked her to get in touch with Sylvain's brother and parents. His parents were away on a trip, and I didn't know how to reach them. My heart sank that I had to give this terrible news.

The two officers would be here in about twenty-five minutes. The dispatcher knew exactly who I needed to be with me at the house. Two officers that I trusted and knew well. I felt relieved that she knew what I needed in that moment without having to tell her.

She would stay on the phone with me until they arrived.

All I could think was that maybe, just maybe, this is just a cry for help. I imagined him sitting there scared and confused and waiting for someone to come help him. How long has he been waiting for someone to come get him? How many hours had gone by since I spoke with him and didn't realize that he was waiting for me to come and help him?

While I was still on the phone with the dispatcher, I texted my brother and my best friend. They both rushed over to my house.

My brother walked in the door all out of breath like he ran over, but I quickly realized it was panic. He was questioning how all this could be happening. How did he not know Sylvain was going to do this when he dropped off the kids and said bye? How did he not realize or pick up on that Sylvain was saying goodbye for the last time to him and the kids in front of his eyes? How could he do this to them? How could he do this to me?

I handed him Sylvain's letter and asked who was with

my kids? His wife, my sister-in-law left work and would stay with the kids until we found out what was going on.

I looked at my cell phone and noticed I had been on the phone with dispatch for about thirty minutes. It felt like two hours. I was crying and panicking by the time the two officers got to my house.

They walked in the door, I ran to both of them and asked, "Did they find him?" They answered, yes, with their eyes lowered.

I asked, "Is it too late?".

Again, they answered, yes.

My brother and I fell to the floor hugging each other and screaming. I was shaking and crying, and said are you sure? The officers said, "Yes, we are so sorry."

I didn't know what to do or what else to say. What other questions do I ask? All that came out of my mouth was: Why? Why? How is this possible? This doesn't make any sense. How could Sylvain had been in such as bad place, and he didn't say anything to either one of us? Why?

I started realizing we needed to tell our families somehow and how difficult that was going to be. I asked my brother to call my parents and sent Sylvain's sister another text message saying they found him, and he was gone. It was too late.

Over the next couple of hours, I had many people show up at my house in complete shock. Police officers, the coroner, my parents arrived from Cornwall, some close friends and within a couple of hours, the OPP had sent me a family liaison person from the wellness unit, a child psychologist, and an inspector to help with planning a funeral.

I asked one of the police officers to please notify a few officers right away that were close to Sylvain. The police officer that Sylvain coached and had a close relationship with was getting married in a couple of days, and I knew this was going to devastate her.

I quickly realized this news was going to spread like wildfire among the First Responder community since Sylvain was so well known.

The resources and support the OPP initially sent were unbelievable, but I needed those resources and support three months prior when there was still a chance for him. We thought we were doing everything we were supposed to be doing so he would get better.

My parents arrived within a few hours and I'm sure they cried the whole two-and-a-half hour car ride to my house, in complete shock and disbelief. They arrived at my house and there were already so many people in my kitchen and living room. Sylvain's parents and siblings planned to come from Montreal the next day and the kids were going to sleep over at a friend's house for the night so we could figure out how we were going to tell them the news. I dreaded this thought.

We sat around my kitchen table for hours in complete shock and trying to process what just happened. We had many discussions about how this couldn't have been for nothing. How could someone like Sylvain who was such an incredible father, husband, police officer and person come to ending like this? It didn't make any sense. We knew we couldn't let him die in vain and quickly turned the conversation to how can we help other families from not having to go through the same tragedy that we are going through. We decided that night that we wanted to share his story and be open about what happened so others could hopefully learn from it.

One officer came to the house that night who was a good friend. Anthony and Sylvain coached our boy's hockey together for a few years and we saw him and his wife at the hockey arena multiple times a week. Anthony looked at me with a sadness I cannot explain. He said he was so sorry, he should have done something. I said to him. "It's ok, you didn't know. Not many people knew Sylvain was off work and was struggling."

"No you don't understand. I feel awful. You see, I've had PTSD for many years but have never told anyone. If I would have just told Sylvain what I have been through, then maybe I could have helped him." Anthony continued, "I look at you now and see the pain this is causing you, and what it will do to your kids. I see my wife in you and realize how easily I could have done this to my own family. I know I need to get myself more help now and don't want to put my family through this."

Anthony hugged me and left. I wasn't sure what he really meant until months later, how Sylvain's death would help others.

The coroner explained to me that he had died of carbon dioxide poisoning in his car, and he had a lot of medication on him. He knew what to do because he had been to so many suicide calls over his career.

A few weeks later, the coroner told me he had purchased the items to rig his car at least two weeks prior to his death and had receipts to prove it. This was very difficult for me to understand. How could he have been planning to do this for at least two weeks prior and not say anything to me? We had been best friends for almost twenty years and the fact that he didn't confide in me when he was in his darkest time, was one of the hardest feelings I've gone through. I believe he planned his death to ensure he wasn't inconveniencing anyone else. He made sure our kids were safe with my brother, my kids were not home when I found his note, he put chicken dinner in the crockpot, and he knew his location wouldn't get dispatched to any of the OPP detachments that he worked at.

If there was one thing that was always consistent about Sylvain – he was organized. He even meticulously planned out his suicide.

11

YESTERDAY, DADDY DIED

A psychologist showed up at my house within hours of Sylvain passing. He told me he was sent to help us out by the OPP. He was there to help us out with anything that we may need assistance with. My biggest concern was how do I tell my kids that their dad has died?

The thought of telling them this crushing news hurt myself and my family to the core. We were going to change their whole entire life with one small message. This was possibly going to be the worst day of their entire life. They were so innocent, naïve, and young, and this was going to be the most painful moment for them. How on earth was I going to break them this news without seriously damaging their souls?

The psychologist and my family then came up with a plan on how we were going to tell the kids the next day that their dad had died. They were going to sleep overnight at a friend's house and my brother would pick them up the next morning and bring them to the house for me.

The psychologist wanted to know each of the kids' personalities in depth and about their relationship with their dad. We went one child at a time explaining each one of their personality's and how much each of them had a special but unique relationship with their dad.

Jacob, who was 10 years old at the time and the oldest, was competitive, loud, liked to be the centre of attention, dramatic, a little self-centred, and a natural leader. He loved to do everything with his dad, and they had a special relationship where Sylvain took him under his wing and taught him so much. Sylvain had been his hockey coach for many years and Jacob was used to having him on the bench encouraging him and giving him tips on how to get better. They loved to fish together, play catch, or watch hockey games on tv.

Nicholas, who was 8 years old at the time had a quieter, more laid-back personality and would go with the flow of anything. Not much bothered him but he followed his big brother around all the time and wanted to be just like him. Nicholas had a special unique characteristic for helping other people, genuinely caring for others, and being great with little kids. Sylvain also coached him for hockey and spent a lot of time encouraging him to do his best at anything. Like Jacob, Sylvain also took him fishing, played sports in our backyard, and watched hockey on tv. Nicholas really looked up to his dad and wanted to be a fan of the Montreal Canadiens too.

Emily, who was 5 years old at the time, had a spunky but very loving personality. She was active and loved talking. She was a complete tomboy from being around her brothers and wanted to keep up with them and everything they were up to. Sylvain also helped her out on the ice and taught her to skate. They had a more loving relationship than the boys. Sylvain loved to read her books and even paint her nails. They also fished together often.

After explaining more about the kid's relationships with their dad, the psychologist then formulated a script of what to say and it had to come from me. He explained that it was important for me to be the one to deliver the news to them. I was not sure I would be able to do it. The thought of crushing their hearts brought me to tears many times while we were planning this pivotal moment. We prepared for any questions the kids would have and how we were going to deal with them. Would they want to know details on how he died? What would we say about suicide? What other questions would they have? Will they cry? Scream? Run out of the house? Hate me? Hate Sylvain for dying?

The psychologist explained how he thought each child would probably react. He said Jacob will probably freak out, maybe scream, and even leave the room. If this happens, I needed to stay in my place with the other two kids, and one of the other family members can walk out with Jacob and give him space. He will probably come back to the room on his own. He said Nicholas probably won't be as dramatic, but he may also follow his brother or ask some questions. He continued that Emily will probably have no reaction and probably will not really know what is happening because she is so young.

The psychologist said if they kids have any questions, it is really important that we do not lie about anything but also don't elaborate. Just answer their questions honestly, with a direct response and let them lead with more questions. I asked how do we answer any questions about how he died if they come up? The psychologist said, you can tell them that daddy was in an accident in his car. Do not say car accident and that way you are being honest, and it will be easier for them to understand and accept. We would not elaborate or explain suicide yet.

I had a script in my head that I ran through in my mind over and over again. Each time, I would start crying and could not imagine the pain I was going to deliver to the three little people that meant the most to me in the whole world.

It had been an extremely long day and night, and it was extremely hard to go to bed that night with no one in the bed beside me. I outreached my arm to the spot where Sylvain slept and felt the emptiness of knowing he was never going to sleep there again. I cried for hours, replaying all the moments of the day, wondering how I was going to get through the next day without Sylvain and tried to fall asleep. This was going to be an impossible task. How do you find peace and calm to sleep after you find out your husband committed suicide?

I woke up the next morning with a pounding headache and could not believe I had actual slept for a bit. For a split second, I thought it was all a dream but when I looked over at Sylvain's side of the bed, I realized it was not and started crying again. My eyes were swollen from the day and night before and I was dehydrated. I dreaded what the day would bring and did not want to get out of bed. How was I going to get out of bed each day completely on my own without him?

My future went black. Tomorrow and the next day seemed like an impossible thought. I was not supposed to live the next days, weeks or years on my own. Sylvain was always supposed to be with me. What about all the plans we had? Our plans for next week while I was on holidays disappeared. What about our family vacation we were going to take the kids on next year? Gone. I could not bear the thought on going on a family vacation without him. We had just celebrated our 14th wedding anniversary a few weeks earlier and decided not to get each other anything because we were finally going to go on a proper honeymoon for our 15th. That was not going to ever happen now. I started to cry again. What about our retirement and our plans to spend our winters down south? Thinking about a future without Sylvain made me lose hope. How was I going to get through anything without him, especially these next couple of days and weeks? These would be the hardest days and he would not be there holding me.

I opened the curtains in our bedroom and squinted at the bright light coming through. I started to focus my eyes and noticed something in our backyard that caught me off guard. At first, I rubbed my eyes to make sure I wasn't seeing things.

There were about 200 black birds all across our lawn.

They were all on the ground and they were hopping towards the house.

I don't have a lot of trees in my backyard, so this was very strange.

"What the heck?" I said aloud.

I yelled to my mom to come and see.

She couldn't believe it.

"You've never seen this many birds before?", she asked.

"No, never.", I answered.

I went to the front yard, and they were all on the grass in the front yard too. None on the lawn across the street or to either side of me at the neighbour's house.

At the time, I just thought it was really neat until a few days later I realized that I have a tattoo on my back and my kids are represented by three black birds. I believe Sylvain knew that that morning was going to be the most difficult days of my life and he gave me a sign to let me know he was with me.

It was a coincidence.

The first of many to come.

I HAD ABOUT 30 minutes to have a shower and get ready before the kids would arrive at the house. I had my parents, my brother and sister-in-law with me, as we sat the kids down on the couch. I knew this was going to be the hardest conversation I would ever have with my kids, and this would change their lives forever.

The kids ran in the house, all excited to tell me about how they had an awesome time sleeping over at a friend's house and how they got to stay up late and watch a movie. They were so happy to see me and gave me hugs.

"Where's dad?" Nick asked and I just ignored his question.

They realized their grandparents were here and were surprised to see them and gave them big hugs too. They had no idea what was about to hit them.

I asked them to come sit on the couch, and I sat on the coffee table in front of them.

"Try not to cry, hold it in for a bit longer" I was telling myself. I felt sick to my stomach and thought I was going to vomit.

I sat in front of them and said what I had rehearsed in my head over and over again the night before. Talk slowly.

"I have something very important to tell you. Yesterday daddy died."

Then we waited for their reactions. My heart sank and my eyes started to swell with tears. My sister-in-law and mom already had tears flowing down their cheeks.

Jacob immediately, stood up, started yelling and screaming "No.... what happened?". It was just like the psychologist said he would react.

I said he had an accident in his car. I hadn't lied but also didn't need to tell him more details.

Jacob said, "Oh...well that makes sense because daddy wasn't sick but what about the other car?"

I said that there wasn't another car. I still hadn't lied but knew that if he thought it was an accident, I didn't need to explain anything else quite yet.

He stormed out of the room crying and my dad followed him, just like the psychologist said.

Nicholas, moved to the coffee table where I was sitting, wrapped his arms around me, and just started sobbing quietly. No questions. His crying was hard for me to hear because it hurt me that I couldn't make his pain go away.

Emily, stayed in the spot where she was, just looked around with no emotion and no expression, just watching everyone else. It was clear she didn't fully understand what was going on. She was just observing everyone else's reactions and everyone else's tears.

A few minutes later, Jacob came back in the room, wrapped his arms around me crying and hugging me and we all sat together in my living room and cried for a few minutes. We all exchanged more hugs and I looked at my parents with an expression of what next? What are we supposed to do now? Was that it? The news had been delivered but now what? So, my dad asked the kids if anyone was hungry and helped get them some breakfast.

The doorbell did not stop all day. Friends stopped by bringing food, hugs and words of support. There was a constant flow of police officers, OPP representatives, and police families I had never met before wanting to offer help. The help, food, cards, gifts, and support was overwhelming, but one thought kept crossing my mind: Where was all this support and help three months ago when we really needed it?

Sylvain's parents, his brother and sister also arrived that day from Montreal. I was extremely nervous for their arrival. How would I face them? Would they blame me for his passing? How do I say sorry? I felt so guilty for not keeping their son and brother safe. How would it make me feel to see them so upset and crying? I didn't want to face them but knew I had to. They made arrangements to stay at a local hotel for a couple of days so we could get things sorted out.

Together, we started planning a funeral.

12

POLICE FUNERAL

I had only been to a few funerals in my lifetime, but this was the first time I was going to have to be quite involved in the planning. I do not wish this process on anyone. It is so exhausting and heart wrenching that it is imperative for anyone having to plan a funeral to make sure they have lots of help and support.

The next day, we had a meeting with an OPP Inspector to discuss funeral options that the OPP could offer.

He said they could have an honour guard, a bagpiper, a motorcycle escort, the coffin draped with the Ontario flag, and he went on and on.

At first, I was really confused.

Finally, I asked, "Don't you only do this for officers when they died in the line of duty?"

"No Sarah, we offer this to any officer, it doesn't matter how they died.", he answered.

That line stuck with me for a while. It didn't matter how he died. I had to think about it for awhile and I repeated that line in my head over and over. "It didn't matter how he died."

I thought – "Yes, you are absolutely right!"

My kids need to see that it didn't matter how he died but the impact he had made during his life.

"Let's do it all," I said. "We need to honour him, and we need the kids to see that he was hero as a police officer in life, not death."

The next day I had a very difficult task to write his obituary. I tried to do some research first. I had never written one before. What do you write for a young person who passes, for a police officer, for someone who committed suicide?

I came across a lot of opening statements such as passed away peacefully or passed away at home or passed away from cancer or other illnesses. I thought why is it that we are not ashamed if someone passes away from cancer but are ashamed if they pass away from a mental illness or suicide?

Sylvain had an illness and died from this illness just like anyone who succumbs to any other illness. I was not ashamed of this, and our family was not ashamed of it either. I knew in my heart that a healthy Sylvain would have never made that same choice to end his life.

So, I had an idea for his obituary and had to pass it by his family to make sure they were ok with it.

Sylvain's dad had previously lost a brother to suicide forty years earlier at a time when no one would ever discuss suicide. Sylvain's brother was a psychologist and had been talking to him weekly trying to help. He asked Sylvain the day before he passed if he was having suicidal thoughts and he told his own brother no. If only Sylvain had opened up to him, maybe his brother could have helped him.

So, his family was absolutely on board with my idea.

I began to write;

Sergeant Sylvain Joseph Francois Routhier, age 37 took his life on Tuesday July 31ˢᵗ, 2018, after a brief battle with a mental illness.

I included a picture of him in his police uniform. When we released the obituary and decided to be open about how he died, it gained a lot of attention from police forces, first responder organizations, and the media. It was a bold statement to be so open about his passing, but I knew that nothing would change if people did not know. I did not want people whispering or asking other people behind our back what happened.

Once we released the obituary, I knew that we would need to have a very difficult talk with my kids about suicide. They needed to hear the explanation from me rather than perhaps a rude comment from kids at school. Again, another conversation I never thought I would need to have with my kids. I felt sick to my stomach again thinking about how we were going to do this.

We consulted with the OPP psychologist again about how we should explain Sylvain's suicide to the kids. It had been a couple of days since the initial conversation of his death, and we had another conversation with just the boys. The psychologist felt Emily would be too young to understand and it was not necessary at the time to give her details. We planned another script which I again memorized in my head and sat the boys down. My parents were there with me for support.

"I need to talk to you guys about some more details about daddy's death" I started.

"Daddy had an illness in his brain called a mental illness that hurt his head. He was in his car and took lots and lots and lots of medicine. The medicine made him fall asleep and his heart stopped. And when you do something that makes your heart stop, it's called suicide."

The kids would understand that you can get really sick from taking too much medication. We did not know for sure if and how much medicine Sylvain took, so for the time being, this explanation would work. We hadn't lied to them about anything, and we did not give more information than was needed.

As the kids got older and if they ever asked more details, then I could explain how I found out later once the coroner's report was released that he died from carbon monoxide poisoning from his car exhaust.

Over the next couple of days, we had a lot of meetings and things we had to put into place. I felt like a walking zombie running on nothing, not being able to eat or sleep. I'm so thankful for my dad's help through these couple of days. He kept notes from all our meetings, and to-do-lists for each day so we could have everything ready for the visitations and the funeral.

Planning involved meeting with the funeral home personnel, ordering flowers, blocking off hotel rooms, deciding on what Sylvain would wear, organizing a video of memories and photos, choosing a casket, deciding on cremation or not, music, speakers, choosing a cemetery, and the list continued.

One of our first meetings with a Catholic Church where we had planned to have the funeral. Sylvain and I were both Catholic but not practising. When we pulled up to the church, there was a large amount of scaffolding due to some renovations that would not allow up to have a proper processional, like we discussed with the OPP. As our meeting continued at the church, I was disheartened to learn about all the rules we had to follow. We could not have his coffin draped with the Ontario flag, we could only have one person speak during the eulogy and it could only be five minutes long. The priest would conduct the longer eulogy. If there was not enough room in the church, any police officers that attended would wait outside to ensure there was enough space for the family and friends. I left the meeting feeling disappointed. This was more about the church than it was about honouring Sylvain's life, but we continued with our plans anyways.

The OPP suggested that we could dress Sylvain in his number one formal uniform which is normally the uniform they would wear for formal ceremonies such as their graduation or funerals. I had only ever seen him in his formal uniform when he first graduating from the OPP in 2005. I knew where his formal uniform was kept in our closet and handed it over to be given to the funeral home. There was one issue. Many of the pieces to his uniform were missing and I could not find them. I was missing his belt, shoes, white gloves, and some special pins.

The OPP inspector told me: "Don't worry, we will make sure he has everything on his uniform that is needed."

We needed to order flowers for the funeral so my dad, Sylvain's dad, his brother and myself went to a local flower shop. I was feeling especially down driving to the flower shop and was trying to hold back tears in front of the men in my life.

We walked into the flower shop and the first thing we all see is a wooden sign with a large daisy painted on it, and the sign says: "Don't Forget Your Roots". All four of us stopped dead in our tracks.

My dad asked, "Are you guys reading this right now?"

This sign was definitely a coincidence or a symbol from Sylvain. His nickname growing up was "Roots" because it was a short version of our last name: Routhier. The daisy also had significant meaning since our wedding flower was daisies. We handed out daisy seeds as wedding favours to all our guests and the wedding bouquets were also full of daisies.

"Don't Forget Your Roots" - I read it again.

It actually put a small smile on my face, the first time I had smiled in days.

I thought, don't worry Sylvain, we could never ever forget you.

My dad bought the sign so I could hang it in my house and ordered a few more so all our family members could also put them in their houses. First the black birds in the yard, the same as my tattoo, and now this "Don't Forget Your Roots" sign - I was starting to believe that his presence was around me.

I started receiving messages from police forces across the province in support of our decision to be open about his suicide and letting us know, their members would be attending the funeral. I was notified that the OPP Commissioner would be attending and would speak at the funeral. I was starting to get nervous about how many people were coming and if we would be able to accommodate everyone at the church. Everything was planned for the visitations and funerals for the next week, and I decide to head to our trailer for the weekend as we normally would and get away for a couple of days.

We pulled into our seasonal campground where we had spent our summers for the past three years. It was a community where we felt at home and the kids wanted to go play with their friends. I needed a break from all the craziness and media attention that was building. Everyone helped us out so much. My brother, who also has a trailer right beside us, took care of feeding us for the whole weekend and other families helped watch the kids when I needed to lay down.

On the Saturday morning, I woke up with a huge feeling of regret. Something about the upcoming funeral that we had planned did not feel right. I walked down to the water, sat in Sylvain's little fishing boat that was on the dock where he spent hours fishing with the kids, and called my dad. There was a really cool mist and fog covering the lake as the sun was rising and I could see two loons not far from where I was.

I told my dad that I think we needed to change the funeral location from the church to somewhere larger that could accommodate as many people that showed up and we needed to make the funeral about Sylvain. He asked me if I had any ideas of where else we could have it.

"I don't know why I didn't think of this sooner, but we should see if we can do it at the local hockey arena, where I happened to work.", I answered.

Since it was August, the ice would be out and it was probably sitting empty. I had the connections and knew who to call and called my director on his personal cell phone. He said of course we can do it and made all the arrangements. I called my dad back and gave him the news that we could move everything to the local arena. It was perfectly fitting for Sylvain. It was where he coached our kids playing hockey, where we watched our billet sons play hockey and the ice where Sylvain himself played hockey for many years. No one would have to sit outside, I could do the eulogy, the commissioner could speak, and whoever else we wanted to be a part of it. I slowly cried some tears of relief as I walked back to the trailer and got back into bed since the kids were all still sleeping and had no idea I had left.

I laid my head down and closed my eyes. I immediately

started feeling a weird sensation that started at my toes and ran through my body to my head. It was like a wave of tingling. Once the sensation got to the top of my head, it moved back to my toes, and then again back to my heads. At first, I didn't know what to think about this wave that was going through my body but it made me giggle, and then it stopped and my lips started to tingle. Just my lips, nothing else. It felt similar to the feeling of having Sylvain's lips pressed against mine when he would kiss me. Was Sylvain kissing me, I thought? Is this possible? This was so weird, but it made me smile and I started to giggle again. I could feel his presence with me once again as I closed my eyes and continued to feel my lips tingling. I laid super still concentrating on the feeling and hoping it wouldn't go away. I knew deep down, it was Sylvain and maybe this was another sign that he was with me, and I made the right decision to move his funeral. To this day, when I've had a rough day, cannot sleep or I am sad and miss Sylvain, my lips will tingle when I lay really still and try to fall asleep. The tingling calms me and I know he is with me.

On the morning of Tuesday August 7th, I asked if I could see Sylvain a few hours before the visitations were to start at the funeral home. It had been a full week and I still had not seen him. I needed some time to see him and then go back home and compose myself before the visitations were to start. I think I needed to feel some closure and see for myself that he was truly gone. Our entire family including Sylvain's parents, his siblings, my parents, my brother and his wife, and my kids headed to the funeral home. We were also trying to decide if we let the kids see him or not?

Again, we consulted with the OPP Psychologist, and his answer was, "Why not? You have been so open with the kids about everything, why stop now? It will help offer some closure for them as well."

I thought, I would see him first and then decide if I think it was ok for the kids to see him.

I was the first to be led into the room where his body lay in the casket. I could tell easily from his side profile that it was him. As I moved closer, I noticed the formal OPP uniform he was in and the white gloves that were on his hands.

I moved closer and all I could say in my head to him was, "What have you done? What did you do to yourself?"

I cried and put my hand on his hands that were folded together on his chest, and felt how cold they were and how his hands felt like stone. Seeing Sylvain's body actual gave me a small feeling of relief. It made me realize he was really gone and gave me some closure. He looked so peaceful, but I felt a calm come over me.

I talked to our other family members once everyone had a chance to see Sylvain, and we decided that it would be ok for the kids to see him. We all entered the room with them and answered any questions they had. It was heartbreaking to see them sad and trying to understand that they will never see their dad again after these moments.

WE WENT BACK HOME and got ready for the first of two visitations. I was nervous, tired and did not want to go through with what I undoubtedly had no choice of doing. A carefully selected group of Sylvain's closest co-workers guarded his casket during the visitations. One stood on each side of him in their formal dress uniform, with their head bowed and their hands clasped in front of them. It added a personal touch that showed his brothers and sisters in uniform were still standing by his side.

The flood of people was overwhelming, and I couldn't tell you today who came and who didn't. I felt like a walking zombie, but I remember the line ups were out the doors and many, many people came in uniforms and many people came from all over our province. I remember a few pivotal moments of people who came that I did not expect such as our City's mayor being one of the first in line, childhood friends of Sylvain's from Montreal, co-workers that he worked with from the Parliament that I hadn't seen in almost 15 years, my bridesmaids from our wedding that I had lost touch with. I remember many tears, many people in shock and disbelief.

Sylvain's parents were overwhelmed with the amount of people who came, who cared and who's lives had been touched by Sylvain. His parents could not believe that officers who did not even know him or worked for other police forces, came to pay their respects. It was unfortunate that Sylvain did not know the impact that he had on so many people when he was alive.

Jacob, my oldest son, came dress shopping with me to pick something to wear for the funeral. We walked around the mall looking in stores and he suggested I wear a black dress that had some flowers on it. He, all of sudden, seemed so grown up and mature. We went into one store, and I tried on a couple of dresses until we found the perfect one. He even chose a matching necklace, and I could tell the store employee that was helping us was wondering what was going on. We told her that we were dress shopping for my husband's funeral. She said I'm so sorry and looked at Jacob and said: "My dad died too when I was 10 years old, and it is not easy. I miss him a lot and I know your dad probably loved you so much."

THE DAY OF THE FUNERAL, I again felt like a walking zombie. I was going through the motions of getting myself ready, doing my hair and makeup, and putting on my dress and trying not to think too far in advance and what the day would hold. I was nervous about my decision to stand in front of so many people and do the eulogy. Would I be able to get out what I planned to say? What if I froze and just started crying? Would I be able to keep myself together? I was nervous about the kids and how this might be a diffi-cult day for them. I was worried that I may have forgotten to plan a detail. I was hoping everything would go as planned.

Our family all went to the funeral home for a small cere-mony, and we got to say our final goodbyes to Sylvain before they closed his casket and draped it with the Ontario flag.

I could not say goodbye. I just whispered: "See you soon". I already knew that his presence was with me and would be in the following days, weeks, and months. We were brought into a room where there were about six men dressed in formal OPP uniforms and I could tell by their medals and fancy epaulettes on their shoulder's that they represented the OPP organization. I was introduced to the OPP Commissioner and the rest of his deputies.

Sylvain and I had only ever once met the OPP Commis-sioner at his police graduation. I thanked them all for attending but did not know what else to say. Do I unleash everything I think their organization needs to change so this doesn't happen again to other officers? I was nervous and decided this was not the time or place but there was a fire in my stomach that I knew I would not be able to silence for long.

We drove to the arena following the hearse and there were police officers on the route saluting us. Well, saluting Sylvain. This was a powerful moment.

The funeral started with Emily walking down the aisle first holding the funeral director's hand, following Sylvain's casket. I slowly walked behind her holding Jacob and Nicholas' hands to the sound of a bagpiper playing *Amazing Grace*.

The arena floor was packed with people. The whole right side with rows upon rows of uniformed officers. I recognized uniforms from many different services including the RCMP, Toronto Police, and others. On the left-hand side, the rows were filled with family and many friends.

We walked all the way up to the front and took our seats. The OPP Chaplain started the ceremony and my stomach was turning because I knew I was going to get up on the stage shortly and speak my mind.

Other speakers during the funeral included the OPP Commissioner, an OPP officer friend of Sylvain's, my parents, and Sylvain's parents. Once all the eulogies were done, the bagpipe's started playing and the pallbearers gathered around Sylvain's casket. They marched over in unison to their spots and slowly started meticulously folding the Ontario flag on his casket. The Ontario flag held a lot of significance. Sylvain devoted his career to serving Ontario communities and it was fitting that they honoured him in this way. I couldn't hold back my tears any longer and the site of Sylvain's close co-workers folding the flag brought up too much emotion. Sylvain's TRU boss, our friend who broke the news to me a week early of his passing, walked over to me holding the folded Ontario flag folded up perfectly and his police hat on top of it. He handed them to me and my arms were shaking.

All the police officers that were in uniform then left through the back door to line up along the road where Sylvain's casket was loaded into the hearse.

It was pouring rain like I had never seen before and I felt bad that they were all standing there getting soaking wet as they saluted Sylvain as he drove away.

13

THE NOTE

About two weeks after Sylvain passed, I had a huge urge to start looking through all of his belongings. I had unanswered questions about why he did this, and I wasn't sure if I would ever find any answers. That's the thing about losing someone to suicide, is you constantly ask yourself: WHY? Why didn't they say anything? Why didn't they ask for help? Why did they feel like ending their life was the best solution? Why? Why? Why?

I started with his night table. I didn't really know what was kept in the two drawers, so I opened the top one and just stared at all the little trinkets. I felt like I was violating his privacy and just looking at what was in the drawer made me feel close to him. These were all the things he kept safe for a reason. There were hockey medals he had received from going to tournaments coaching the kids, some of his watches, cards I had given him over the years for birthdays or anniversaries, some special homemade pictures and cards the kids had given him, some pictures, cigars, OPP flashes, and other things that he clearly did not want to throw out. It was hard going through the items and thinking about him and the memories we made over the years.

I started to cry, then I got angry and mad at him. Again, the thoughts of how he could do this to me and leave me like this surfaced. I stopped, took some deep breaths, got some Kleenex, and opened the second drawer.

This one was filled mostly with books he had received as gifts or had read and wanted to keep. One on the story of Theo Fleury, who was a hockey player that had been abused, one on how to train like a navy seal, and another one called American Sniper which was the story of Chris Kyle, who was a highly decorated sniper who ended up being murdered by a former marine who had PTSD. I'm not sure why I flipped through all the pages of the books, one by one, checking to see if there was a photo used as a bookmark or something else.

The last book on in the bottom of the drawer was called "Hockey Drills and Skills". It was a book I had given him as a present many years earlier when he started coaching hockey. It was a thick book with many options and drills he could use during practice. I flipped through the pages and all of a sudden, a folded white piece of paper fell out and landed on the floor. I picked it up thinking it must have been some rough scribbles of drills he wanted to use.

I unfolded it and was shocked. It was addressed to me in Sylvain's handwriting.

"Sarah my love, I am so sorry ~~for~~ to have come to this point but I can't live like this and continue to make you ~~fur~~ suffer while I'm still around. You have been an amazing wife that's been so supportive. I don't want to do this to our beautiful family but I have no choice. I love our kids Jacob, Emily and Nicholas so much and I really don't want to do that to them but I have no choice. Please hug them lots for me. I love you so much Sarah. You

brought me joy for so many years. I can't see you taking care of me anymore. Tell your family I love them. Please tell my family I love them all as well.

Sylvain"

Oh my goodness, I was freaking out. What was this? Did he mean for me to find this? Was this his original note that he was going to leave for me and then he decided to write another one and leave that one instead? He felt like he had no other choice? He didn't want me to take care of him any longer? These statements were crazy!!! I started pacing around and landed on the floor crying. So many thoughts were going through my mind. I found some answers, but it just led to more questions. I wish I could talk to him and set him straight. I wish I could turn back time and do something more to stop him from feeling this way. All our conversations that we had in the weeks before his passing came flooding back to me. Did I ever say anything to him that it was too hard for me to take care of him? No, I don't think so. Did I ever make him feel like he had no other choices? No, definitely not. Geez....I was lost and I re-read the note again.

His initial suicide note that I found on the day he passed was very harsh, and it did not sound like the Sylvain I knew and loved for so many years. They were the words of an illness. This second note was very loving and the Sylvain I knew and there was even a difference in his handwriting. His handwriting in this note seemed calmer and the letters were not as distorted or sharply written as the first.

After a few days, I started packing away some of his belongs but did not feel a strong urge like I needed to find something like previously. I started some keepsake bins of many of his things that I am sure the kids would want someday. We had some quilts made for the kids out of his clothes and some very special teddy bears made out of his police uniforms. As I was packing some things away, I came across a blue duffle bag up on our loft in our garage. I assumed it had some baseball equipment in it but when I opened it, it was all the missing pieces to his formal dress uniform. Everything was in the bag! His shoes, gloves, belt, and special pins. I wondered why he would have kept them in a separate bag hidden away? And, go figure that I would find everything just a few weeks after I was looking for everything. In the bottom of the duffel bag, I found something that gave me goosebumps. There were small brochures from every police funeral he had attended in his career. Now this made sense. This was his duffel bag he grabbed when he had to go to a funeral. I flipped through the brochures and saw many names of officers that I recognized that had died in the line of duty. I remembered watching their funerals on tv and I was now actually friends with some of their widows from a group we belonged to. I bet Sylvain never thought that the next funeral where he would wear these special items in the duffel bag, would be for his own.

Shortly after his passing, I knew I needed help trying to navigate my grief and figure out how to keep living. Anyone who has lost someone to suicide will understand that there is another level of grief attached to suicide. You constantly beat yourself up over how did you not prevent this from happening. You replay the weeks, days, and hours before your loss trying to figure out what you missed. It can be excruciating and exhausting and very hard not to place blame on yourself. I had regular conversations with my brother about this and for weeks we talked about and replayed so many moments leading up to his passing. My brother also had a huge amount of guilt and we felt like we were going through similar struggles with trying to come to grip with what Sylvain had done.

I attended a suicide bereavement peer support group through the Canadian Mental Health Association which helped me understand a lot of my feelings surrounding Sylvain's death.

It was really difficult to go through this type of therapy, but it helped to know that I was not alone. Other families had also lost loved ones to suicide, and it helped to talk about Sylvain and explain to others what he was like. It can both be happy and extremely sad to talk about him. There were some days where I did not want to go because I knew it was going to bring up some tough emotions but after attending, I felt better. I learned a lot from this therapy and one of the most impactful things that stuck with me was this: someone contemplating suicide has a form of tunnel vision and can only think of ending their own pain. That was a perfect way to explain it. Sylvain had such a deep level of pain in his head that he couldn't think straight and couldn't think about anything other than ending his pain. He could not think of the consequences of ending his life or how it would affect me or our children for the rest of our lives.

Often people think or say: "How could someone leave their kids like that?" I truly do not think he knew what impact that would have on our kids. Even though my last time speaking with him was the day he left, his last words to me, his kids and our family was to make sure everyone knew he loved them.

14

MEDIA ATTENTION

W hen I decided to be open about Sylvain's passing and his struggle, I was not prepared for the media attention that followed shortly after his funeral.

Two other OPP officers also took their own lives within a three-week span, and it was all over the news. My heart sank each time an officer friend called me to tell me the news. I couldn't believe this was happening to other families. It was extremely difficult to know that other people were living the same tragedy I just had been through just a few weeks earlier. I'm not sure what made the other families also be open about how their loved ones passed, but it must not have been an easy decision. I credit them for their openness and believe that if they had not done that, then all the change and awareness that was about to come would not have happened.

The headlines read: *"Force 'deeply devastated' as three OPP officers commit suicide in three weeks"* [1]

The headlines created attention and pressure on the OPP and questions needed to be answered.

News stations started contacting me wanting to get my thoughts and opinions on the matter. At first, I was really nervous but then I thought that I could try to make a difference and bring awareness by allowing people to hear my perspective and story. I decided to speak to the media and do interviews because I felt it is harder for people to understand what suicide looks like if you have not lost someone previously in that way. I thought from what I had been through and in hindsight, that so many things needed to be changed in the first responder world and maybe my voice could help people, help make a difference and help create change. This was in my way how I could take what I learned from the tragedy of losing Sylvain and turn it into something good for others. I would be able to make sure he did not die in vain and for nothing.

There certainly is a stigma that exists around mental illnesses in first responders and surely this would be a first step to eliminating the stigma. A stigma in my opinion is really just people not understanding a circumstance or not getting all the information so they can properly understand it.

Stigmas are heightened when people are not open about them and no one wants to talk about a situation. Suicide is definitely an exceedingly difficult topic to speak about because for the family you feel like you should have prevented it from happening which in turn, can bring shame and guilt.

Over the next week or so, I did many interviews in person, on film, on the radio, and over the phone. Luckily in my volunteer role as a Water Safety Ambassador with the Canadian Red Cross, I had previous media training. I learned how to speak about difficult topics such as a drowning, while remaining calm and composed. I somehow wondered if this was a weird coincidence that prepared me for this moment.

Shortly after, the OPP commissioner held a media conference announcing to launch an internal review of their entire mental health programs and admitted that their police force needed to do more for their members mental health. The plan would include management travelling across the province to hold round table meetings with officers, retired officers, family members and widows or widowers. The commissioner hoped that people would come forward with what challenges or barriers they faced, and the organization could make changes.

At first, I was skeptical that this was going to be a lot of open-ended promises for change, and nothing would really come out of it, especially when the commissioner then retired shortly after the announcement. However, a few months later I got my chance to speak my mind about what I thought needed to be changed when deputies came to my house to interview me for my round table meeting. My brother attended too for support and had some great suggestions also. I had a few sheets of paper prepared ahead of time with my list which included such things as better access to experienced psychologists, teaching family members or spouses about PTSD and what signs and symptoms to look for, allowing them to have easy access to OPP resources and support, and making it easier for their members to reach out for help. They wrote down everything I said and after they left, I started shaking and crying. It was difficult to rethink about all the things that we had been through and what could have saved Sylvain.

A few months later, the Chief coroner's office of Ontario also released to the media that they did an investigation into the nine police officer suicides that occurred in 2018, including Sylvain's. When the Chief coroner called me himself to interview me for this investigation, he explained to me that it is his office's job to look into any death that occurs that seem outside the normal realm and nine police deaths in one year exceeded what was considered normal. He asked me many questions, and again I was able to voice what I thought could have been implemented previously that could have saved Sylvain.

The OPP's commissioner's report was released a few months later. I was surprised, nervous, and excited that a report was actually put together. It was incredibly detailed and stated they had interviewed more than 350 people that came forward who wanted to contribute their experiences, good or bad, in order to make change. The report announced 150 recommendations of things that needed to be changed within the OPP in order to remove the barriers and stigma around mental health. It was bittersweet that it was recognized that so many things needed to change, but yet it was too late for Sylvain. The recommendations included change around a huge variety of policies within the OPP including everything from the hiring and promotional processes to easier access to trained psychologists, from the return-to-work process to how to provide families with knowledge and support and include them, from looking at their peer support programs, websites, and response to a member suicide to memorializing members who have died. It was very comprehensive, and I felt like many of the things I could identify after the fact for areas of improvement, were put into this report. I was then asked to sit on the Commissioner's Healthy Workplace Advisory Board which was developed with many stakeholders to ensure the recommendations were carried out. I felt completely honoured and could witness and make comments on many of the changes that would take place within the OPP. It felt like Sylvain had a voice.

Shortly after, the Chief Coroner's Report was released with 14 recommendations for police forces in Ontario to change. The recommendations included items such as better access to experienced psychologists, ensure proper staffing so officer's do not get overworked, and a policy to keep track of any first responder suicides along with a review committee for each death.

Each time there was an announcement or a media release regarding these topics, the media would contact me again asking for my story, a statement, or an interview. Before I knew it, over the course of a year and a half, I had participated in about 20 interviews. It started to get very tiring and emotionally draining to bring up the pain of what I had gone through. I kept doing them because I thought if I could just reach one person and someone could learn something from me, then maybe a life could be saved.

A friend who was a paramedic contacted me asking if I would consider speaking to a group of local paramedics about what I had been through and if I could offer any advice. He thought that by sharing my story, it would possibly help paramedics that were struggling be able to acknowledge that they too may need help or at least make their mental health a priority. I was extremely nervous but had a lot of experience speaking in front of groups over the years. From a young age, I used to do the readings in church, at weddings or funerals, I spoke at drowning prevention conferences, and led staff training sessions. I had no problem speaking in front of many people, but this would be different. I was going to let strangers into a very vulnerable and personal story that included a lot of emotion and trauma.

I tried to prepare and think about what I wanted to talk about. I would start with describing who Sylvain was as a husband, father, and police officer, then I started to talk about his career and how he started struggling. Then, I would go through the details surrounding his passing. How much detail did I want to share? I thought. I guess I'll see what feels natural as I am speaking. I hoped that I wouldn't start crying.

This first talk went better than I expected. The story came naturally for me, I did have some emotional moments where I tried to keep it together but what made it so amazing were the comments, thanks and hugs I got after. People told me how much my story resonated with them and how much I was making a difference. I was told to keep sharing my story because it would have an impact and help so many. That was my ultimate goal the day Sylvain died, and I decided I wanted to help others. It felt good to be able to take a tragedy and be able to help others learn from it.

Soon after, other people and organizations must have heard that I was doing keynotes and sharing my story. I don't think there are many people out there willing to talk so openly about suicide. I started talking at OPP detachments to members and their families, the local college, first responder conferences and at treatment centres, and local mental health events. My "Speech" developed the more I did it and evolved to also include photos on a slideshow. Each time I had a talk approaching, I would get nervous and worry about what the audience would think or how they may react. I had people leave the rooms crying before because they could relate or something in what I had been through made them realize that they needed help.

The only problem was that it was extremely draining on me. I relived the day Sylvain died each time I spoke about it.

I would often shed a few tears when I talked about certain parts of the story but for the most part could keep myself together. But when I was done, left, and was alone driving home, in my hotel room, or on a plane, I cried hard. It was difficult to balance - how much did I want to expose myself? How much was I willing to relive the pain, just so that I could hopefully touch and save one person? There must be another way to be able to get this story out to people that would not be so draining and emotional on me. And then it came to me, I needed to write a book.

15

LESSONS LEARNED

I often get asked – What do you think is the one thing that caused all this from happening?

That is an extremely difficult question to answer, but my answer is - it wasn't just one thing.

It was a whole magnitude of many things and stress is the main root of it all. We all of have stress in our lives and we have times when our stress levels are higher than others.

Picture your life as a giant cup and each bit of stress, or circumstance, or challenge in your life, slowly fills that cup with a drop of water.

Personal stress could be unresolved issues from your childhood, moving away, getting married, starting a new job, financial concerns, buying a house, paying a mortgage, taking a trip, a loved one becomes ill, relationship turmoil, more financial concerns, retirement stresses and parenting - which should be a whole paragraph on its own!

Then add to that your work stressors – everything from showing up on time, being prepared for your shift, finishing paperwork, going on calls, maintaining your skills, maybe it's coaching a new team member, going to a difficult call or seeing trauma.

For First Responders, add; re-living the trauma that they've seen on the job and then pretending that seeing those things is supposed to be normal. It's an expectation to live up to the badge that is on your shoulder that never leaves you. Even when you go home at night. Each day, each shift, each call, you're adding small drops of water to your cup. And your cup will keep filling and filling.

How are you emptying your cup?

I'll tell you what Sylvain did. Nothing.

He tried to empty the water out of his cup by working out a lot, he would drink sometimes, he would get away with his buddies like going to the police international hockey tournament, we went on family vacations, and he coached kids' hockey. It was too little, too late.

Fourteen years of police work and personal life stresses filled his cup of water to the very top. Then, moving to a new detachment and starting a new job as a Sergeant, made his cup overflow and spill.

Combine work stress and personal life stresses that have been simmering for a long time and have not been dealt with, along with lack of awareness, knowledge, resources, and support - once these stresses became too much, IS what happened to him.

So, how do we prevent this from happening again?

Another extremely difficult question to answer because it is different for everyone, whether you are a first responder yourself, a spouse or family member or in charge of a first responder organization. So here are my thoughts broken down and I should remind you that I am not a professional doctor in this field, just an experienced widow.

To First Responders:

Firstly, thank you. I know you all chose the profession you are in because you wanted to help other people and make a difference. You all have huge hearts and have made an incredible sacrifice to devote your career to servicing others. You have also made a huge sacrifice that there is potential for you to get injured on the job. Don't forget that you can also get mental injuries because of your job, and these are much harder from all aspects because they are unseen.

I should clarify that to me a First Responder is anyone who serves others in a time of need whether you are a nurse, a doctor, in the military, corrections, border security, paramedic, fire or volunteer fire, dispatchers, bylaw officer or police officer and more. It truly takes special people to help others in their worst moments and put others before themselves and their families; and to me, that what makes you all heroes. But heroes need to take care of themselves too. They have feelings, can break, and can ask for help too.

Secondly, speak to someone today. You need to educate yourself and find resources and support for your mental health now. Do not wait until you can no longer handle things. Start seeing a counsellor now to prevent what could happen and find a councillor that is experienced in dealing with First Responders and trauma. I do not care if you are into your first year of your career, retired, think it is a waste of time or you do not think you need to speak to someone. I can guarantee that you need it. Just like you put in the time and effort into your physical health, you need to do the same for your mental health.

If I could do it all over, I would have encouraged Sylvain to see a councillor regularly throughout his career. Every six months, after a traumatic call, and whenever he needed to talk to someone. Allow a family member or spouse to go with you and be in the room with you. You can sign a waiver allowing them to be with you, which is something I only found out after Sylvain passed away. When I got his medical records, and read through all his appointments with his psychologist, I realized he was not telling his psychologist everything that he should have been. He did not tell her about the nightmares, the trauma he had experienced at work, about the change in his anger, his paranoia or any of the changes that I noticed in him. His psychologist did not know the full picture and when Sylvain came home from his appointments, he could not remember a lot of what was discussed with him. If he had cancer, I would have been allowed with him through all doctor appointments. I would have known what the diagnosis was, what the treatment plan was, what signs and symptoms to look for if things got worse, and what do to about them if they did. You need to advocate for yourself!

Take check of yourself and notice if you are experience things or doing things that are not normal for you. Are you having trouble sleeping, feeling more tired, easily irritated, getting headaches, muscle tension, or no longer want to be social? These can be some of the first signs that something is not right. If these symptoms persist, try to minimize your stress, get plenty of rest, take time off if needed. And don't use the excuses: I can't because we won't have enough people to work, work is too busy, I have to go to court, I signed up for a course, or anything else.... this is not your problem to fix, it's your organization's!

I heard these excuses for many years when Sylvain was feeling stressed but did not want to take time off, exercise, eat right, or speak to a councillor.

Are you experiencing anxiety, sadness, disturbed sleep,

fatigue, aches, and pains? Noticing a decrease in your performance at work? Withdrawing from friends, loved ones or your spouse? Upset or angry at the world? Getting into arguments more frequently or turning to unhealthy coping mechanisms? Drinking more? Any one of these signs is giving you a signal that you need help. Please don't try to hide it, ignore it, or think things will just get better on their own. They won't and they will probably get worse if you choose to do nothing. Again, speak to a councillor, find out what supports are available through your workplace, take time off, and lean on your friends, co-workers, family, or spouse for support. They are all in your life to help you and support you through anything. If you were diagnosed with cancer, would they all be there to help you? Of course, they would, and a mental illness should be no different. It is an injury that you cannot see like cancer, you did nothing to bring it on yourself and you should not be ashamed of it.

If a co-worker goes off work, treat them like they have just been diagnosed with cancer. Reach out regularly, ask them if they need anything, stop in, bring food, organize a staff fundraiser for them, help get their kids to activities, help get them to appointments, or offer to meet for a coffee. The worst thing you can do for someone struggling with a mental illness is ignore them. Could you imagine if you had just been diagnosed with a brain tumour and all your co-workers just ignored you? If no one reached out, you would feel completely crushed like no one cared, which we know is not the case. I get that it can be awkward, and you might not know what to say. Just be honest, show that you care, and offer help. And don't stop reaching out to them. You never know, you might be the one on the other side of the equation someday.

There is something else I want you to know that Sylvain

did not know. Recovery and getting back to work is possible! Do not lose hope. Sylvain did not know anyone who was diagnosed with a mental illness or PTSD that came back to work because no one spoke about it. He lost hope for his career and his identity as a police officer. I would encourage those who have been through a diagnosis and recovery, to be open about it and talk to others. Your openness and wiliness to share what you have been through will help your fellow co-workers, family, or friends.

If you are in a really bad place, I want you to know: No matter what your thoughts may be telling you, you are never a burden to your loved ones, and they could never be better off without you. No matter how bad your symptoms get, or how difficult things may be, your pain can be temporary and please do not make a life changing decision on something that is temporary. You will be easing your own pain, but that pain will be transferred to your parents, your spouse, your children, your family, your friends, and your co-workers. There is help, you can recover, and I can tell you that I will be dealing with the ramifications from Sylvain's suicide until the day I die, and so will my kids. This is so unfair to put this trauma on kids. You are loved, and you do have another choice. Please see the end of this book for a list of resources and support or talk to someone today.

The organizations you are working for need to do so much more. The change is happening, but it is slow, and you need to advocate for that change for yourself and your co-workers.

To First Responder Spouses, or Family Members

There is no question that your job as the everyday person who supports a First Responder is extremely difficult. For many years, I always thought my role as a First Responder spouse was to make sure I was able to handle or take care of everything in our lives, to make his job at work the easiest possible. I didn't want Sylvain to worry or stress about our home life. I knew he had enough on his plate with his job. I planned my work schedule around his, I made sure the house was quiet or we were gone when he had to sleep during the day, I was supportive when he wanted to move to another city for job advancements or be away to take courses or go to training sessions, I took care of the laundry, cleaning, groceries, finances, meals, kid's activities, planning vacations, birthdays, or family gatherings. I constantly worried about him getting injured on the job or worse, dying in the line of duty. Let's face it, I kept our household together and worked full-time too!

I know you are all doing the same and you are all the unsung heroes that support your First Responder too. There is one major thing I missed for 13 years of his career. I never thought that PTSD or suicide would happen to him. It was never on my radar whatsoever. So, I'm here to tell you a hard truth. It can happen to you and to your First Responder before you know it. It is more of a possibility that they could develop a mental illness than dying in the line of duty, so you need to educate yourself now.

Read above to learn the signs and symptoms of mental illnesses in your First Responder. You will probably be the first person to notice changes in them. Talk to them, support and encourage them to get help, seek counselling, or take time off if needed. Go to the appointments with them and be involved in their recovery plan. I wish I had advocated harder to do this for Sylvain.

Find out what resources and support their workplace offers now, before you really need the help. Make sure as the spouse or family member, you have access to those resources and support. Find out the websites, phone numbers, benefit plans, and who to talk to if you start to notice changes in your person. Find a good councillor that has experience working with first responders and trauma. Know what programs are out there, talk to others, reach out if you need help. Find support groups for yourself and your First Responder. I've included a list of resources and support at the end of this book, but every workplace is different and may have additional supports as well.

What I can tell you is when I was in it, when Sylvain was struggling, I felt like I had nowhere to turn to. I looked up things but just couldn't believe that this is what we were going through. I may have been in a bit of denial. It can be very hard to navigate what the proper avenues are to help them get better. I didn't want to interfere with his career and was worried about the career ramifications for him, but looking back now, it may have saved him. Follow your gut, your instincts, and remember what can happen. I was blinded by the shock and did not know how desperate or how bad Sylvain was. I did not encourage him to take care of his mental health like he did with his physical health throughout his whole career. He never saw a councillor once, until he already had suicidal thoughts. This is an important preventative measure that you should not ignore.

To First Responder Organizations, Associations, and Decision-Makers

Are you creating a workplace that fosters a healthy environment when it comes to your employee's mental health? How do you accomplish that? Do you have proper resources, support, and training in place for your first responders AND their family members? What do you do when an employee needs help? Do you have a peer support program, and do you have the right people in those positions? How are employees who come to you with a mental illness treated and supported? What is the follow up if someone is off work? How do other employees treat them? Are there stigmas present in your organization? What does your organization do if you lose an employee to suicide? Do you have a way of memorializing those employees who have died? I would encourage you to take some time to answer these questions and to look at your mental health programs in your workplace. Is there more you could be doing?

If you really want to make a change, I suggest you read the Chief Coroner's Report on Police Suicides in 2018 as well as the Ontario Provincial Police Independent Review Panel: Final Report. Both links are provided in the resource section of this book.

Even though the reports only studied police deaths, it can certainly apply to every organization that is represented today.

The action items from the reports include but are not limited to:

- normalizing mental health challenges and removing the stigma
- assistance with transitions with new positions or the return-to-work process
- involving family and spouses in prevention, care, benefits, resources and return to work processes
- access to experienced health care professionals
- maintain appropriate staffing levels to avoid burnout
- manage with sensitivity any situations of breach of duty or care where a member faces charges or public embarrassment through mainstream or social media

- access to private walk-in support and peer support groups
- relook at your benefit limits, and examine recovery options and support

I would encourage you to take the lead in your organization in making a difference and placing as much importance on your employee's mental health as their physical health. If your organization has already lost someone to suicide, you will know how devastating the effects are. First responder organizations spend an incredible amount of money and resources on training and preventing deaths on the job, the same should be done for deaths because of the job. They are unfortunately more likely to occur, and the statistics need to change. There is so much more we can all do together to ensure not another First Responder dies because of suicide.

EPILOGUE

As you finish reading this book, all I can ask is that you remember Sylvain and look at your own life and take care of yourself and those around you. Don't be afraid to speak up, ask for help, slow down, find healthy coping strategies and recognize that others might need some understanding too. That staff member that always shows up late or that co-worker that loses their temper, or a friend who become withdrawn; ask them if they are ok.

You never know what someone else is going through. Let someone know if you are having a bad day, talk about it, do something for yourself or speak to a counsellor.

ALTHOUGH MANY PEOPLE can handle a lot of stress with no issue for many of years, if you let that stress accumulate, it can affect your sleep, your judgement, your patience, your physical and your mental health.

· · ·

I RECOGNIZE that my story may have hit close to home or brought up some emotions. It's ok! Don't be afraid of your emotions or feel ashamed. Ask your neighbor if they are ok. Offer a hug or feel free to speak to a friend. I hope that sharing my story has helped you with a better understanding about mental illnesses and the stigma that exists surrounding suicide. Don't be afraid to talk about it or seek help.

POSTSCRIPT - MOVING FORWARD

Jacob, Nicholas, Emily and I have been rebuilding our lives.

I KNOW Sylvain's death will affect each of the kids at different times in their lives and in different ways. They have taught me the most about being resilient and that resiliency doesn't mean we ever forget him as we move on with our lives. They all see a grief counsellor regularly and I'm trying to teach them from an early age that it ok to speak to a professional at any time.

There are definitely heartbreaking moments with them; when they miss their dad or wish they could tell him about the big fish they just caught or about the tooth they just lost.

Father's Day this year was especially difficult when they made him gifts at school and delivered them to his grave site.

If you are struggling or know someone who is struggling, please know that you are never a burden to your loved ones. Visiting a gravesite would be a much larger burden to those you love.

SHORTLY AFTER SYLVAIN and the two other OPP officers passed away, a group of friends and colleagues of Sylvain's decided to host a golf tournament and raise money for the families who had lost a loved one. I participated in the tournament and was blown away by the support and people that came, including the new OPP Commissioner. It was a huge success, and many people were asking if they would do it again the following year, so they agreed to make it an annual event. I wanted to be involved in helping plan the next events and had an idea to help other people using the fundraising money, so we created the Sylvain Routhier Memorial Foundation. The Foundation's mission of prevention and education focuses on supporting families and children whose parents have been victims of PTSD related deaths, supporting first responders in need who are suffering from PTSD who will benefit from otherwise inaccessible programs, and support for bursaries to aid deserving students in their studies related to trauma support of first responders, or to pursue careers as first responders. We went on to also host an annual hockey tournament and have helped facilitate fundraising events and scholarships for other first responder families who want to honour their loved ones.

I DONATED the outdoor rink Sylvain built in our backyard to the local neighbourhood where we moved and with the help of some businesses and many volunteers, we had the official grand opening of the Sylvain Routhier Community Rink in 2019. It was amazing to see our kids as well as all the local neighbourhood kids enjoying the rink he built for the past couple of winters.

The last couple of years without Sylvain has obviously been extremely difficult. I have found more strength than I ever knew I had, and the truth is, we all have it inside ourselves. You will find your strength too when faced with adversities and you will have no other choice.

WE HAVE HAD to adapt to a new normal and I have had to figure out how to get up every day and keep living. I definitely have harder days than others and am learning to recognize my own stress levels and when I need to slow down and take time to myself. Life tends to get extremely busy, and we can easily forget what is important in life and what our priorities should be. Adapting to a new normal has been the most difficult. I choose what I want to be involved in, make space for myself, and recognize when I need to slow down. I have learned how to take care of all the things he used to do especially maintaining a home, a trailer, and a boat. I have learned to lean on my close family and friends to get me through birthdays, Christmases, special occasions, and anniversaries.

IT'S BEEN difficult to become a lone parent and have all the responsibility of three kids solely on my shoulders. This is very different than being a single parent in that I do not have another person to help with anything and am responsible for them 100% of the time. I never get a break from being the parent and it can be very exhausting to try to make all the decisions on my own, get kids to all their hockey, and navigate the things kids go through such as teenage drama, emotional breakdowns, difficult situations, or fights among each other. I have found that, in times of need, I can lean on my friends, family, and hockey community.

ABOUT A YEAR after Sylvain's passing, I made a very difficult decision to leave my career. Although I tried going back to work part-time after a few months and then returning completely to full-time, it was really difficult to take on being the sole parent, being able to focus on my job, work evenings and weekends and be on call. My job no longer accommodated my priorities and I needed to make my kids the main priority. I miss the comradery that came from working with people but decided to go back to school and get a diploma in Business Administration. I hope to return to work someday when the time is right for me and my kids.

I have been blessed with other opportunities that help me to heal. Knowing that I am helping others in some way, helps me feel like I am making a difference. I have been involved in pursuing recognition for officers who have died by suicide both at the OPP level and Ontario level. Memorializing and honouring officers who have died by suicide is important to me because I believe they should be recognized for their years of service to our community. Don't forget, it didn't matter how they died.

THE EXTREME LONELINESS that came after Sylvain's passing was something I was not prepared for. I lost my best friend who I spoke to about everything. Every single detail about my life, my days and my kids and the emptiness and grief that I experienced is indescribable. We moved within a few months to the house we had planned on purchasing on the day Sylvain passed and have already outgrown it. I met an incredible man through a good friend, who has become my support system, my best friend, and a stepdad to my kids. He also has two kids so we are moving again to a larger house that we can make our own for our five kids.

I WAS NOT EXPECTING to fall in love again or to have to keep living without Sylvain, but what I learned is that I will never fully move-on. I thought that grieving had a timeline and one day I would just be over it and be able to possibly date again and my heart would heal. I was wrong! Grieving most definitely does not have a timeline. I will grieve Sylvain until the day I die but I have learned that my heart is capable of growing to love someone else at the same time that I'm grieving Sylvain.

I WOULD HAVE NEVER WISHED for Sylvain's life to end this way. I wish it could be different. But, while I wouldn't wish for this, I do try to see the blessings in it. I have found that when I need Sylvain most, I can still find him. I think about what he would do or say in tough situations that I have to face. I can still hear his voice when needed. I know he guides me and still kisses me at night when I cannot fall asleep. Also, every time I see a black bird or get goosebumps, I know he is sending me a sign.

· · ·

A SMALL PART of me thinks sometimes that this was meant to be. Sylvain had an impact on everyone he worked with or met, and if suicide can happen to Sylvain, then it can happen to anyone. I think this is the message, it can happen to you if you don't take care of yourself. Don't forget your "Roots". Don't forget why you got into this profession. Don't forget where you came from. Don't forget why you support and love a first responder. Don't forget to support and love others. Don't forget what can happen.

I SEEK COUNSELLING STILL when I have rough times and I have built friendships with other widows that have been through something similar. The support I get from these groups of friends have probably been the most beneficial in my healing. We try to focus on all the good memories we have of Sylvain and we speak about him often in our house and around our friends and family. I feel that I have started to build his legacy that my kids will be proud of someday, through the foundation and helping others and being open by sharing his story. My hope is that they will be able to hand out the scholarships and awards at the graduation ceremonies some day, and be proud of the police officer that he was, and how he is still helping others.

I HAVE LEARNED that building resilience takes a lot of time and patience and I try to focus on all the positive blessings I have in my life. I used to complain in a joking way that none of our three kids looked like me, and now I know why. It is so I can see Sylvain in each of one of them. I can see the twinkle of Sylvain's eyes every time I look into Jacob's eyes, and he definitely also has his competitiveness. I can see

Sylvain's smile every time I look at Nicholas, who also has his calmness and caring spirit towards others. I can hear the kindness of his laugh whenever I hear Emily laugh, and she definitely looks the most like him with her dark hair and dark brown eyes. With these reminders, I know Sylvain is still with me and will live on in our kids forever.

EULOGY

Good afternoon et Bonjour à tous,

I want to start by thanking everyone for being here today. The support we have received for our family in the last couple of days has been overwhelming and we really appreciate all of you taking the time to come here today to celebrate Sylvain's life.

Most of you here will remember Sylvain and periods in our lives when our paths crossed. Some will remember him as a police officer, or a hockey teammate, some a close friend, a neighbour, a family member who liked to dance at weddings, or a coach. I'm sure you are all talking about him and remember the great times and sharing childhood, work, camping, fishing, hockey stories and more.

The story I want to share with all of you, is our love story. It started almost 20 years ago. We met in high school at the age of 18 through a mutual friend. At first it was a friendship and then it turned to love. Our first date was to the movies and afterwards we sat in his hockey billets car and talked for hours. During that talk, he eventually worked up the nerve to ask in his cute French accent: "Would you like to be my girlfriend?" I was drawn to his shyness, his sense of humour, his caring heart, his energy, his athleticism, and he sure was attractive! Now I have to tell you that at this time, he and his hockey teammates had just bleached all their hair blonde and he had one of those awful mushroom cuts. I remember at one hockey game, while he was on the ice playing, his mom showed me a picture of him with his natural hair colour, and I thought "oh wow, he's actually better looking than I thought!"

He attended my high school prom, and we did the long-distance thing while he was pursuing police foundations in Montreal and I went to College in Ottawa. We made a point to see each other every single weekend taking turns traveling back and forth.

We soon realized we could no longer be apart, and he switched to Algonquin College in Ottawa so we could be together. The day he proposed, he brought me to the top of Monte Royal in Montreal, got down on one knee and of course I said yes. At only the age of 21, we were scared to tell our parents we got engaged and thought they would talk us out of it. Instead, they gave us their support and love, and they must have known we were right for each other. Just to clarify to Jacob, Nicholas, and Emily – no one is getting married until at least 30!

On June 26th, 2004, we were married in Cornwall in a small ceremony surrounded by our closest friends and family. We lived in Ottawa and had no clue what marriage was really about, and he wanted 6 kids. He worked at the house of parliament at first as a security guard, and then shortly after was promoted to Prime Ministers Detail which entails escorting the Prime Minister around parliament. We knew it was just a matter of time before a police force would want him. The day we got the phone call that he had been hired by the Ontario Provincial Police was one of Sylvain's proudest moments. It was one of many to come.

Jacob was born in 2007, Nicholas arrived less than 2 years later, and Emily completed our happy family in 2012. I think then he realized 6 kids would be A LOT! Sylvain was so excited to be a dad and couldn't wait to pass down his passions to our children. And boy, he sure did.

They were all on skates by the age of 3 and he spent hours in the freezing cold every winter building them an ice rink in our backyard. In fact, at the top of our wish list when purchasing our current home, was a very large, flat back-yard, with no neighbours close by, to avoid any flying pucks. He let me make all the decisions about the rest of the house we built. At first the rink started out small enough with just a liner and some water. He did lots of research and over the years it has expanded to 55 feet by 35 feet, full size walls all around all sides, taller on the ends, spotlights for at night, benches, a homemade water Zamboni contraption and even a ramp for the snow blower. He would dress up in goalie equipment and let the kids take shots on him for hours. We had annual hockey games for our kid's teams on that rink and Sylvain even had his own hockey buddies over on occasions to play 3 on 3. He also made the kids a mini-stick hockey rink in our basement and a full wood wall with a net and targets painted on it so the kids could take shots with real pucks!

Hockey is a huge part of our lives, even though I've never played! When Sylvain moved to Ontario around the age of 16 to play junior hockey, he was billeted by some wonderful families. He always wanted to give back to other families, like they had done for them. We had 2 billet sons over the years, Brett Wely-chka, who was the last captain of the Belleville Bulls and Brandon Macham, the Picton Pirates goalie. They both became an extension of our family and like big brother's to our kids. Sylvain took our kids to many of their hockey games and both Brett and Brandon helped out on the ice with our kids teams.

The last couple of years the boys have been playing rep hockey and in one more year, Emily will probably also be following in their footsteps. To all our hockey family friends who have asked if they can help this past week, this is when I will really need your help! Sylvain was an assistant coach or trainer or just helped out on the ice whenever needed for all 3 of our kids. 6am practices, tournaments, and fundraisers, he always found a way to help. Our winters are spent at hockey arenas and our summers are spent camping.

We enjoyed travelling and camping at different campgrounds all over the province. The kids learned to fish, kayak, roast marshmallows, catch frogs, snakes and bugs and enjoy the outdoors. I remember a particular camping trip where we were camping just north of Orillia, he got called out with the TRU team, and a TRU team member came and picked him up at the campsite. He left me at the campsite alone with 2 young boys under the age of 3 and I had to take down, pack and hitch up a tent trailer all on my own. We now have a seasonal trailer!

Sylvain loved his job with the OPP, and we moved around the province so he could do what he loved. We lived in London, Corunna, Petrolia, Orillia, and Amherstview before moving to Belleville for my job! The hardest decision for him was deciding to leave the TRU team. The kids were getting older, and he wanted to coach them and be with them more often. He often missed birthdays, special occasions, hockey games and even almost missed my brother's wedding! No matter what he wanted to do with his career, I supported and encouraged him.

I can only imagine how shocking this news about Sylvain was for most of you, and you are probably all wondering "how did this happen." Anyone who knew Sylvain will tell you what an incredible person, police officer, brother, uncle, son, husband, and father he was. He was laid back, easy going, calm under pressure and loved to joke around, even at his own expense. He loved fishing, camping, golfing, making and taste testing beer and of course, he loved the Montreal Canadians. Another passion he passed on to Nicholas. Jacob is a Chicago Blackhawks fan, which was our billet son, Brett's fault. And Emily has yet to choose her favourite team.

In April, Sylvain started struggling with depression and anxiety and had to take time off work. He was getting help and had a lot to work through. Many years of accumulated work-related stress, difficult calls and lack of sleep had come to a head. He had never once complained about being stressed or that a certain call bothered him. I asked him often if he wanted to talk about work, but he kept many difficult things from me, in order to protect me.

Sylvain will continue to live on in everyone that he touched. Especially our children.

Jacob who is 10 years old, has his competitive spirit, is very protective of his siblings and is definitely a leader!

Nicholas who is 8 years old, has his calm demeanour, loves to joke around and play pranks and is very thoughtful towards others.

Emily who is 5 years old, loves to laugh, has her father's energy, and looks most like him.

Jacob, Nicholas, and Emily, I promise to remind you every day about how much your daddy loved you. We have a wonderful support system from the OPP, my work friends with the City of Belleville, our hockey friends, our Lake Avenue friends and our family. We will be OK.

As for the rest of you, 1st responders, family, and friends. I ask that when you leave here today, talk about Sylvain. Take a look at your own life and please do not be scared to speak up if you are struggling with a mental illness. Speak to someone and know that it is ok to ask for help. Speak to your co-workers, friends, a councillor, or your spouse. I would also ask that police forces and other first responder organizations please ensure that those people have the resources available to help when someone comes to them. Suicide is not something our family is embarrassed about because we know this will not define Sylvain. If we can just help prevent this from happening to one other family by sharing Sylvain's story, then that is all we can ask for. We want to bring awareness about mental illness, PTSD and suicide. Please help us to do this by continuing to share and talk and keep Sylvain's memory alive.

Thank you

STATISTICS & RESOURCES

Statistics

  In Canada:

- Approx. 11 people die by suicide each day
- Approx. 4,000 deaths by suicide per year
- 1/3 of deaths by suicide are among people 45-59 years
- Suicide is the second leading cause of death among youth and young adults (15-34 years)
- Suicide rates are approx. 3 times higher among men compared to women[1]
- First Responders experience Post-Traumatic Stress Disorder and Critical Incident Stress at 2 times the rate versus the general population. It is estimated that over 70,000 Canadian first responders have experienced PTSD in their lifetimes. [2]

- 11 percent of First Responders have reported suicidal thoughts as a result of the job. [3]

- During 2018, nine deaths by suicide occurred among serving and retired police officers in the province of Ontario, including Sgt. Sylvain Routhier. This number was thought to be unprecedented. [4]

Resources
The Sylvain Routhier Memorial Foundation
https://sylvainrouthierfoundation.com/

To Contact Sarah:
info@sylvainrouthierfoundation.com

Ontario Provincial Police Independent Review Panel: Final Report
https://www.mcscs.jus.gov.on.ca/english/ Policing/OntarioProvincialPoliceIndependentReviewPanelF inalReport.html

Staying Visible, Staying Connected, For Life: Report of the Expert Panel on Police Officer Deaths by Suicide
https://www.mcscs.jus.gov.on.ca/english/ Deathinvestigations/OfficeChiefCoroner/ Publicationsandreports/StayingVisible.html

Canadian Mental Health Supports

Crisis Services Canada: 1-833-456-4566 or text 45645
Suicide prevention and support
Hope for Wellness Help Line: 1-855-242-3310
Offers immediate mental health counselling and crisis intervention to all Indigenous peoples across Canada
Canadian Mental Health Association 416-646-5557

Offers programs, peer support, information on various mental illnesses, and links to local resources

https://cmha.ca/

Canadian Association for Suicide Prevention 1-613-702-4446

Provides information and resources to communities to reduce the suicide rate and minimize the harmful consequences of suicidal behaviour.

https://suicideprevention.ca/

Ontario Mental Health Supports

Ontario Drug and Alcohol Helpline: 1-800-565-8603
Ontario Mental Health Helpline: 1-866-531-2600
Ontario Problem Gambling Helpline: 1-888-230-3505

Centre for Suicide Prevention 403-245-3900

An education centre, offering workshops, events and resources

www.suicideinfo.ca

https://www.suicideinfo.ca/resource/first-responders-trauma-intervention-suicide-prevention/

First Responder Resources
OPPA Encompass
1-866-794-9117

Access to personal and family wellness programs, children and seniors-focused support services, virtual care support, crisis intervention specialists and mental health treatment facilities https://www.encompascare.ca/ and OPP Beyond the Blue OPP Beyond The Blue focuses on the wellbeing of family members through education, tools, and ultimately building a community that understands what it's like to live with and/or love a police officer. Together, we will keep an open conversation about all things police-life so that we can create real change at home and on the front lines. https://www.oppbeyondtheblue.com/

Canada Beyond the Blue

A peer-led, non-profit organization with Chapters across the nation. BTB is dedicated to strengthening and supporting families of law enforcement officers in Canada.

https://www.canadabeyondtheblue.com/

Wounded Warriors Canada

1-888-706-4808

Wounded Warriors Canada is a national mental health service provider utilizing clinical best practices and evidence-based care to create an environment of compassion, resiliency and hope for Canada's Veterans, First Responders and their families.

https://woundedwarriors.ca/

Boots on the Ground

1-833-677-2668

This dedicated team provides confidential and anonymous Peer Support 24/7 to First Responders across the Province.

https://www.bootsontheground.ca/

Public Services Health and Safety Association

1-877-250-7444

PSHSA is ready to help employers establish their PTSD

Prevention Plans and Programs since we have extensive experience in the first responder community.

https://www.pshsa.ca/emerging-issues/issues/ptsd

The Mane Intent

1-705-295-6618

This unique equine experiential learning program is tailored to meet the needs of first responders and healthcare frontline who are experiencing job-related occupational stress injuries.

https://themaneintent.ca/equine-wellness-for-first-responders-and-frontline-heathcare-the-mane-intent/

First Responders First

Information about prevention, intervention and recovery and return to work related to PTSD Prevention for first responders.

http://www.firstrespondersfirst.ca/

Badge of Life Canada

A peer-led charitable volunteer organization committed to supporting police and corrections personnel who are dealing with psychological injuries diagnosed from service.

https://badgeoflifecanada.org/

Canadian Critical Incident Stress Foundation

1-289-239 - 7978

The CCISF is a national charitable organization dedicated to the mitigation of disabling stress and the fight against Post Traumatic Stress Disorder.

https://www.ccisf.info/

Treatment Centres

The Haven Mental Health Treatment Centre
905-713-7231
Providing occupational-specific inpatient/outpatient mental health care exclusively for First Responders and Uniform Personnel
https://www.thehaven.cloud/

Project Trauma Support
A Canadian program that addresses Post Traumatic Stress and Operational Stress Injury in military personnel, veterans and first responders.
https://projecttraumasupport.com/

Homewood Health Centre
1-866-932-0037
A specialty inpatient program focused on treating individuals struggling with substance use and concurrent disorders. AMP also offers specialized streams for healthcare professionals and for first responders, military, and veterans.
https://homewoodhealth.com/health-centre

Edgewood Health Network Treatment Facilities
Offers programs designed to specifically address the addiction and mental health concerns of the most heroic members of our communities: military service members, veterans, and first responders.
Facilities are Edgewood in Nanaimo, BC
1-866-414-5857
Bellwood in Toronto, ON
1-866-671-0075

Clinique Nouveau Depart in Montreal, QC

1-866-422-1870

https://www.edgewoodhealthnetwork.com/

Trafalgar Addiction Treatment Centres

1-855-972-9760

Provides the best possible care for those who have served in the military or as first responders.

https://trafalgarresidence.com/military-first-responders-rehab/

The Stable Grounds

1-905-717-5921

A privately owned and operated therapy centre, providing residential 30, 60 and 90 day programs for First Responders and Uniformed Professionals who suffer from Post Traumatic Stress Injury (PTSI).

https://thestablegrounds.com/

The LA VIGILE therapy home

1-581-742-7001

A non-profit organization whose mission is to help women and men wearing uniforms or any other adult with problems. Offers professional services on six (6) components: addictions, depression, post-trauma (PTSD), anxiety, anger and letup.

https://lavigile.qc.ca/en/

The Tema Foundation

The Tema Foundation is a non-profit organization that focuses on mental health and wellness for frontline workers, first responders, healthcare professionals, public safety personnel, and the important people in their lives.

https://www.tema.foundation/

US Resources

National Suicide Prevention Lifeline 1-800-273-8255

Veterans Crisis Line 1-800-273-8255, then press 1, or text 838255

Crisis Text Line, text HOME to 741-741

Samaritans USA
A registered charity aimed at proving emotional support to anyone in distress or at risk of suicide through the United States.

http://www.samaritansusa.org/index.php

All Clear Foundation Supporting First Responders
We are convening, amplifying and funding innovative programs to improve the life expectancy and wellbeing of First Responders – no matter their branch, location or resources.

https://allclearfoundation.org/

NOTES

14. Media Attention

1. https://nationalpost.com/opinion/christie-blatchford-force-deeply-devastated-as-three-opp-officers-commit-suicide-in-three-weeks

Statistics & Resources

1. Government of Canada, Stats Can, July 2019 https://www.canada.ca/en/public-health/services/publications/healthy-living/suicide-canada-key-statistics-infographic.html
2. Wilson, Stuart, Harminder Guliani, and Georgi Boichev. 2016. "On The Economics Of Post-Traumatic Stress Disorder Among First Responders In Canada". Journal Of Community Safety And Well-Being 1 (2): 26-31. https://www.journalcswb.ca/index.php/cswb/article/view/6.
3. Canadian First Responder Suicides Stress Vital Need For Support". 2016. Disaster-Resource.Com.
   http://www.disasterresource.com/index.php?option=com_content&view=article&id=2404.6
4. Ministry of the Solicitor General, **Staying Visible, Staying Connected, For Life**
   Report of the Expert Panel on Police Officer Deaths by Suicide, September 2019
   https://www.mcscs.jus.gov.on.ca/english/Deathinvestigations/OfficeChiefCoroner/Publicationsandreports/StayingVisible.html

SYLVAIN ROUTHIER MEMORIAL FOUNDATION

Foundation Purpose:

On July 31st, 2018 after a brief battle with a mental illness, OPP Sergeant Sylvain "Roots" Routhier, age 37, took his own life. Sylvain was an incredible father, husband, and police officer. Sylvain's passing has greatly affected his family, friends, community and many first responders. This foundation was created by those family and friends to help raise awareness about mental health and the stigma that surrounds it.

Our hope is to prevent this from happening to other families through fundraising efforts which will:

• Support families and children whose parents have been victims of PTSD related deaths

• Support first responders in need who are suffering from PTSD who will benefit from otherwise inaccessible programs

• Support for bursaries to aid deserving students in their studies related to trauma support of first responders, or to pursue careers as first responders.

www.sylvainrouthierfoundation.com

ABOUT THE AUTHOR

Sarah is a hockey mom, entrepreneur, and mental health advocate. She is the Founder and President of the Sylvain Routhier Memorial Foundation -

(www.Sylvainrouthierfoundation.com),

the Vice President of OPP Beyond the Blue

(www.oppbeyondtheblue.com),

and sits on many committees including the OPP Commissioner's Healthy Workplace Advisory Group, and the Ontario Heroes in Life Memorial.

Sarah spent her career advocating for Drowning Prevention as an Aquatics Coordinator, as well as teaching part-time at various Colleges, however, she changed her career focus in the last couple of years to make her three kids, Jacob, Nicholas, and Emily her main priority.

Sarah wrote this book to share her very raw story to raise awareness about suicide and mental health illnesses in first responders. Her goal is to prevent this tragedy from occurring to other families and to make change within first responder organizations.

Sarah currently lives in Belleville, Ontario with her new husband and their combined five kids. In her free time, she can be found at the hockey rink watching her kids or at her trailer in Prince Edward County.

www.ingramcontent.com/pod-product-compliance
Lightning Source LLC
Chambersburg PA
CBHW050726030426
42336CB00012B/1423